THE NIXON-KISSINGER
FOREIGN POLICY:
OPPORTUNITIES
AND CONTRADICTIONS

PACEM IN TERRIS III

Volume I
The Nixon-Kissinger Foreign Policy:
Opportunities and Contradictions

Volume II
The Military Dimensions
of Foreign Policy

Volume III
American Foreign Policy in the
Age of Interdependence

Volume IV
The Requirements of
Democratic Foreign Policy

The Nixon-Kissinger Foreign Policy: Opportunities and Contradictions

Edited by
Fred Warner Neal and Mary Kersey Harvey

Volume I of four volumes edited from the proceedings of
PACEM IN TERRIS III
A National Convocation to Consider
New Opportunities for United States Foreign Policy,
Convened in Washington, D.C., October 8-11, 1973, by
the Center for the Study of Democratic Institutions

Center for the Study of Democratic Institutions
2056 Eucalyptus Hill Road
Santa Barbara, California 93108

Library of Congress Catalog Card Number: 74-78889
ISBN Cloth Set 0-87182-100-1
ISBN Cloth Vol. I 0-87182-101-X
ISBN Paper Set 0-87182-105-2
ISBN Paper Vol. I 0-87182-106-0

Designed by Barbara Monahan.
Printed in the United States of America.

Acknowledgments

The Center for the Study of Democratic Institutions gratefully acknowledges financial support for *Pacem in Terris III* from the Businessmen's Education Fund, and from the more than 4,000 Center members who sent special donations or attended the Washington sessions. Dissemination of the proceedings through television broadcast was made possible by grants from the IBM Corporation to the National Production Center for Television, and from the Frances Drown Foundation to the Center.

Harry S. Ashmore
President

Contents

Introduction

Perhaps not since the founding of the Republic has there been such an urgent need for a national dialogue on American foreign policy. Epochal changes in the nature of the world have eroded the old landmarks. Americans of all political persuasions agree that the Cold War foreign policy we have followed since the end of World War II necessarily is giving way. But what is to take its place remains unclear and ill-defined in an international setting in which we can no longer readily identify our allies and adversaries. New and old tensions abroad confront us, while, at home, we must face up to serious economic dislocations, critical shortages of resources, and a crisis of confidence in the national leadership.

These matters made up the agenda for the *Pacem in Terris III* Convocation called in Washington, D.C., by the Center for the Study of Democratic Institutions in October, 1973. At the opening session, Henry A. Kissinger, in his first major address to an American audience since taking office as Secretary of State, warned: "Opportunities cannot be hoarded; once past, they are usually irretrievable." That admonition was clearly on the minds of the eighty-two statesmen, scholars, businessmen, scientists and journalists who for the next three days addressed themselves to consideration of the United States' national interests as they must now be defined in a new global context.

The Convocation was the third in a series taking its title from the historic encyclical, *Pacem in Terris* (Peace on Earth), issued by Pope John XXIII in 1963. John advanced a moral and philosophical argument for co-existence, with a small "c," and his eloquent message also constituted a Macedonian cry for sane foreign policies based upon genuine dialogue among ideological adversaries. The Pope addressed himself not only to his own Church, and the Western world in which it has its roots, but to all mankind. In 1965 in New York, and in 1967 in Geneva, the Center organized international gatherings to explore the practical implications of the moral imperatives identified by Pope John in the context of the new world coming into being in the last quarter of the twentieth century.*

Pacem in Terris III departed from the multi-national composition of its predecessors to concentrate on the comparatively narrow focus of the United States' changing role in the world. With the passing of the Cold War era, the great issues of international economics, thermonuclear deterrence, military alliances, and transnational development were no longer abstractions ordinary Americans would be content to consign to the foreign ministries. In the Fall of 1973, their by-product in the form of a devalued dollar, the sudden scarcity of essential resources, and spreading unrest in the so-called third world intruded into the White House and the halls of Congress, the board rooms of the great corporations, and finally into the average American's living room.

At a time when its decision-making processes are in serious question, the Federal establishment is called upon to forge a new foreign policy in a global setting no longer dominated by the two superpowers who confronted each other at the end of World War II. Europe has become a

---

*See Appendix for details on the previous *Pacem in Terris* Convocations, including the full list of participants in the Washington, D.C., Convocation, October 8-11, 1973.

power in its own right, so has China, and so has Japan. For the first time, the great nations seem to be perceiving—albeit sometimes dimly—that their national security cannot be achieved by constantly increasing their armaments, and that world order can no longer be maintained through military intervention. For national interests to have real meaning in an increasingly inter-dependent world they must be correlated with multi-national and transnational interests.

Yet, at the same time, the international political structure made up of sovereign nation-states survives, even though beset by stresses that can only be described as anarchic. The Middle Eastern War, breaking out on the eve of *Pacem in Terris III,* provided a poignant reminder that the promise of world order has not yet broken through the prospect of armed conflict, actual and potential. If the hoped-for world is less dangerous, the real world still must deal with the real danger of international confrontation, not perceptibly lessened beneath the lengthening shadow of the great powers' burgeoning thermonuclear stockpiles.

Any re-examination of American foreign policy must begin with recognition that the post-war era in international relations combined the worst of nineteenth century nationalism with the most advanced of twentieth century technology. The United States backed into the great *impasse* known as the Cold War, and for the first time became dependent upon a huge, permanent military establishment, without any real public debate on the central issues. It is only now that we have begun to recognize that the result has been to saddle the nation with a foreign policy clearly out of popular control.

The remarkable response to the call for *Pacem in Terris III,* which attracted attendance of more than four thousand persons from all parts of the country, may be seen as evidence of a widespread demand for a full public airing of the life-and-death decisions of foreign policy, for open and candid discussion of alternatives, of optimum goals, and the more likely realizable ones. Practical choices always involve moral choices, and in the United States moral purpose and foreign policy traditionally are perhaps more closely intertwined than elsewhere. Consideration of the national conscience is inescapable as we go about establishing new priorities for our international relations.

Pacem in Terris III was designed to initiate an uninhibited discussion of these matters which would fairly reflect the full range of views now current in political and intellectual circles. The major foreign policy analyses, and the ensuing sharp debates about them by distinguished and expert participants, provide a kaleidoscopic overview. The object, as defined by the Center's Chairman, Robert M. Hutchins, is to "bring home to every American the question about what his country ought to do about the basic issues of life and death."

This is the first of four volumes containing material presented at *Pacem in Terris III* in the form of addresses and recorded dialogue. Volume I focuses on the Nixon-Kissinger foreign policy as it presently exists, the prospect and implications of American-Soviet détente and the nature of the national interest as it must be defended and advanced in the new global setting. Subsequent volumes will deal with the national interest and military power, including our fallible alliances; such transnational issues as trade, development, technology, and the role of the United Nations; and the domestic requirements for a democratic foreign policy, including the problems of secrecy, the roles of the Executive and Congress, and the impact of the mass media.

I

THE POLICY OF DETENTE

In opening Pacem *in* Terris III, *Robert M. Hutchins emphasized the inseparability of foreign and domestic policies. This was to be a dominant theme during that part of the Convocation devoted to consideration of how American foreign policy is, and should be, formulated.*

Two principal, and frequently opposed, formulators of policy dealt with the issue in formal addresses. Secretary of State Henry A. Kissinger and Senator J. William Fulbright, Chairman of the Senate Foreign Relations Committee, offered brilliant analyses of the requirements of global foreign policy, agreeing on much, but differing on fundamentals when they came to the question of how our national interests should be defined and implemented. Both spoke against the immediate backdrop of the war in the Middle East which flared only two days before.

Secretary Kissinger and Senator Fulbright were in complete accord on the desirability, indeed the necessity of proceeding to cement a détente with the Soviet Union. Sharply differing with them, Senator Henry M. Jackson, Democrat, of Washington, later delivered a hard-hitting, emotionally-charged attack on the Nixon-Kissinger détente policy, demanding that any trade concessions or easing of the U.S. military posture be coupled with

1

pressures to force liberalization of certain Soviet domestic policies. Favoring détente, but seeing valid points on both sides of this issue, Marshall D. Shulman, director of the Russian Institute of Columbia University, presented an analysis, in depth, of our new relationships with the Soviet Union and with China.

Neither Slave Nor Master Be

Robert M. Hutchins

This is the time when it is essential that we face the future, not the past. But as a member of the generation now shuffling from the scene, I may perhaps be permitted to take one brief, backward glance at what we have been through. The past is strewn with the wreckage of our illusions.

From the White Man's Burden to Manifest Destiny to the Big Stick to Making the World Safe for Democracy to Containment of the Monolithic Communist Conspiracy to the Domino Theory, the slogans that inspired us seem lifeless now. Certainly they are no longer inspiring.

I will not say that some of them were without meaning or utility in their day. But their day was short, and their effects were at best, as Disraeli used to say, "shrouded in the dark shadows of dubiety." Sometimes they were catastrophic.

It is odd that sensible men once thought it sensible to cry, "Hang the Kaiser!" We hanged him, to all intents and purposes, only to have one worse than he arise. We then had to hang *him*. His place was taken immediately by Stalin and his successors, who could be held in check only by the overwhelming military and economic might of the United States.

We seem to have been the victims of misplaced faith in power, the power of arms and the power of money. As things have turned out, our expenditures on arms have helped discredit our money. And this combination has prevented us from doing at home what common decency demands. I invite you to compare the recent record on appropriations for the poor, the sick, and the elderly with that on military appropriations. The first are inflationary and to be condemned as such. The second are inflationary but indispensable nevertheless.

We appear committed still to the illusion that a country is strong only if it has more and more destructive weapons than its actual, potential, or imagined enemies. I suggest that the strength of a country may depend more upon the strength of its convictions—upon the character and intelligence of its citizens; upon its sense of unity in a national purpose it understands—than upon the bombs it has accumulated. This is especially true if it cannot use the bombs unless it wants to commit suicide in the process. In the meantime, we might remember that justice is the cement that holds society together. If injustice in this country tears it apart, our arms and money will be useless.

We appear to be approaching the end of an era, one to which we can say farewell without regret. The war in Indochina seems to be coming to an end. Mr. Nixon and Mr. Kissinger, amid the applause of all parties, have opened the way to new relationships with the communist world. New relationships should mean new opportunities.

Mr. Fulbright forcefully made the point fifteen years ago that foreign and domestic policies were inseparable. They are manifestly so, even to the most casual observer, today. We must, therefore, look for new opportunities at home as well as abroad. The task is to reassess our policies, to reallocate our resources, to re-examine our goals, and to disenthrall ourselves. Otherwise, "peace with honor" will turn out to be another illusion.

I suggest as a basic postulate of our inquiry the words of Abraham Lincoln, "As I would not be a slave, so I would not be a master." This is a hard saying. Mastery is a simple and attractive idea. To live with other people without wanting to master them when you suspect they want to master you is a challenge to patience, good will, understanding, and courage. But if the world is to be a livable habitation for mankind no other course is open.

The American Experiment is what they used to call it when this country, with a new form of government, new ideals, and new hopes was first established. I suspect that new opportunities for foreign policy may be discovered not in new ways of applying national power but in the revitalization of the American Idea.

Robert M. Hutchins is Chairman of the Center for the Study of Democratic Institutions.

The Nature of the National Dialogue on Foreign Policy

Henry A. Kissinger

The need for a dialogue about national purposes has never been more urgent. Dramatic changes in recent years have transformed America's position and role in the world:

— For most of the postwar period, America enjoyed predominance in physical resources and political power. Now, like most other nations in history, we find that our most difficult task is how to apply limited means to the accomplishment of carefully defined ends. We can no longer overwhelm our problems; we must master them with imagination, understanding and patience.

— For a generation, our preoccupation was to prevent the Cold War from degenerating into a hot war. Today, when the danger of global conflict has diminished, we face the more profound problem of defining what we mean by peace and determining the ultimate purpose of improved international relations.

— For two decades, the solidarity of our alliances seemed as constant as the threats to our security. Now, our allies have regained strength and self-confidence, and relations with adversaries have improved. All this has given rise to uncertainties over the sharing of burdens with friends and the impact of reduced tensions on the cohesion of alliances.

— Thus, even as we have mastered the art of containing crises, our concern with the nature of a more permanent international order has grown. Questions once obscured by more insistent needs now demand our attention: What is the true national interest? To what end stability? What is the relationship of peace to justice?

It is characteristic of periods of upheaval that to those who live through them, they appear as a series of haphazard events. Symptoms obscure basic issues and historical trends. The urgent tends to dominate the important. Too often, goals are presented as abstract utopias, safe-havens from pressing events.

But a debate to be fruitful must define what can reasonably be asked of foreign policy and at what pace progress can be achieved. Otherwise it turns into competing catalogues of the desirable rather than informed comparisons of the possible. Dialogue degenerates into tactical skirmishing.

The current public discussion reflects some interesting and significant shifts in perspective:

— A foreign policy once considered excessively moralistic is now looked upon by some as excessively pragmatic.

— The Government was criticized in 1969 for holding back East-West trade with certain countries until there was progress in their foreign policies. Now we are criticized for not holding back East-West trade until there are changes in those same countries' domestic policies.

— The Administration's foreign policy once decried as too Cold War-oriented is now attacked as too insensitive to the profound moral antagonism between communism and freedom. One consequence of this intellectual shift is a gap between conception and performance on some major issues of policy.

— The desirability of peace and détente is affirmed but both the inducements to progress and the penalties to confrontation are restricted by legislation.

— Expressions of concern for human values in other countries are coupled with failure to support the very programs designed to help developing areas improve their economic and social conditions.

— The declared objective of maintaining a responsible American international role clashes with nationalistic pressures in trade and monetary negotiations and with calls for unilateral withdrawal from alliance obligations.

It is clear that we face genuine moral dilemmas and important policy choices. But it is also clear that we need to define the framework of our dialogue more perceptively and understandingly.

Foreign policy must begin with the understanding that it involves relationships between sovereign countries. Sovereignty has been defined as a will uncontrolled by others; that is what gives foreign policy its contingent and ever incomplete character.

For disagreements among sovereign states can be settled only by negotiation or by power, by compromise or by imposition. Which of these methods prevails depends on the values, the strengths and the domestic systems of the countries involved. A nation's values define what is considered just; its strength determines what is possible; its domestic structure decides what policies can in fact be implemented and sustained.

Thus, foreign policy involves two partially conflicting endeavors: defining the interests, purposes and values of a society and relating them to the interests, purposes and values of others.

The policy-maker, therefore, must strike a balance between what is desirable and what is possible. Progress will always be measured in partial steps and in the relative satisfaction of alternative goals. Tension is unavoidable between values, which are invariably cast in maximum terms, and efforts to promote them, which of necessity involve compromise. Foreign policy is explained domestically in terms of justice. But what is defined as justice at home becomes the subject of negotiation abroad. It is thus no accident that many nations, including our own, view the international arena as a forum in which virtue is thwarted by the clever practice of foreigners.

In a community of sovereign states, the quest for peace involves a paradox: the attempt to impose absolute justice by one side will be seen as absolute injustice by all others; the quest for total security for some turns into total insecurity for the remainder. Stability depends on the relative satisfaction and, therefore, also the relative dissatisfaction of the various states. The pursuit of peace must, therefore, begin with a pragmatic concept of coexistence—especially in a period of ideological conflict.

We must, of course, avoid becoming obsessed with stability. An excessively pragmatic policy will be empty of vision and humanity. It will lack not only direction, but also roots and heart. General De Gaulle wrote in his memoirs that "France cannot be France without greatness." By the same token, America cannot be true to itself without moral purpose. This country has always had a sense of mission. Americans have always held the view that America stood for something above and beyond its material achievements. A purely pragmatic policy provides no criteria for other nations to assess our performance and no standards to which the American people can rally.

But when policy becomes excessively moralistic it may turn quixotic or dangerous. A presumed monopoly on truth obstructs negotiation and accommodation. Good results may be given up in the quest for ever elusive ideal solutions. Policy may fall prey to ineffectual posturing or adventuristic crusades.

The prerequisite for a fruitful national debate is that the policy-makers and critics appreciate each other's perspectives and respect each other's purposes. The policy-maker must understand that the critic is obliged to stress imperfections in order to challenge assumptions and to goad actions. But, equally, the critic should acknowledge the complexity and inherent ambiguity of the policy-maker's choices. The policy-maker must be concerned with the best that can be achieved, not just the best that can be imagined. He has to act in a fog of incomplete knowledge without the information that will be available later to the analyst. He knows—or should know—that he is responsible for the consequences of disasters as well as for the benefits of success. He may have to qualify some goals not because they would be undesirable if reached, but because the risks of failure outweigh potential gains. He must often settle for the gradual, much as he might prefer the immediate. He must compromise with others, and this means to some extent compromising with himself.

The outsider demonstrates his morality by the precision of his perceptions and the loftiness of his ideals. The policy-maker expresses his morality by implementing a sequence of imperfections and partial solutions in pursuit of *his* ideals.

There must be understanding, as well, of the crucial importance of timing. Opportunities cannot be hoarded; once past, they are usually irretrievable. New relationships in a fluid transitional period—such as today—are delicate and vulnerable; they must be nurtured if they are to thrive. We cannot pull up young shoots periodically to see whether the roots are still there or whether there is some marginally better location for them.

We are now at such a time of tenuous beginnings. Western Europe and Japan have joined us in an effort to reinvigorate our relationships. The Soviet Union has begun to practice foreign policy—at least partially—as a relationship between states rather than as international civil war. The People's Republic of China has emerged from two decades of isolation. The developing countries are impatient for economic and social change. A new dimension of unprecedented challenges—in food, oceans, energy, environment—demands global cooperation. We are at one of those rare moments where, through a combination of fortuitous circumstances and design, man seems in a position to shape his future. What we need is the confidence to discuss issues without bitter strife, the wisdom to define together the nature of our world as well as the vision to chart together a more just future.

Nothing demonstrates this need more urgently than our relationship with the Soviet Union. This Administration has never had any illusions about the Soviet system. We have always insisted that progress in technical fields, such as trade, had to follow—and reflect—progress toward more stable international relations. We have maintained a strong military balance and a flexible defense posture as a buttress to stability. We have insisted that disarmament had to be mutual. We have judged movement in our relations with the Soviet Union, not by atmospherics, but by how well concrete problems are resolved and by whether there is responsible international conduct.

Coexistence to us continues to have a very precise meaning:

— We will oppose the attempt by any country to achieve a position of predominance either globally or regionally.

— We will resist any attempt to exploit a policy of détente to weaken our alliances.

— We will react if relaxation of tensions is used as a cover to exacerbate conflicts in international trouble spots.

The Soviet Union cannot disregard these principles in any area of the world without imperiling its entire relationship with the United States.

On this basis we have succeeded in transforming U.S.-Soviet relations in many important ways. Our two countries have concluded an historic accord to limit strategic arms. We have substantially reduced the risk of direct U.S.-Soviet confrontation in crisis areas. The problem of Berlin has been resolved by negotiation. We and our allies have engaged the Soviet Union in negotiations on major issues of European security, including a reduction of military forces in Central Europe. We have reached a series of bilateral agreements on cooperation—health, environment, space, science and technology, as well as trade. These accords are designed to create a vested interest in cooperation and restraint.

Until recently the goals of détente were not an issue. The necessity of shifting from confrontation toward negotiation seemed so overwhelming that goals beyond the settlement of international disputes were never raised. But now progress has been made—and already taken for granted. We are engaged in an intense debate on whether we should make changes in Soviet society a precondition for further progress—or indeed for following through on commitments already made. The cutting edge of this problem is the congressional effort to condition most-favored-nation trade status for other countries on changes in their domestic systems.

This is a genuine moral dilemma. There are genuine moral concerns—on both sides of the argument. So let us not address this as a debate between those who are morally sensitive and those who are not, between those who care for justice and those who are oblivious to humane values. The attitude of the American people and government has been made emphatically clear on countless occasions, in ways that have produced effective results. The exit tax on emigration is not being collected and we have received assurances that it will not be reapplied; hardship cases submitted to the Soviet Government are being given specific attention; the rate of Jewish emigration has been in the terms of thousands where it was once a trickle. We will continue our vigorous efforts on these matters.

But the real debate goes beyond this: Should we now tie demands which were never raised during negotiations to agreements that have already been concluded? Should we require as a formal condition internal changes that we heretofore sought to foster in an evolutionary manner?

Let us remember what the most-favored-nation question specifically involves. The very term "most-favored-nation" is misleading in its implication of preferential treatment. What we are talking about is whether to allow *normal* economic relations to develop, the kind we now have with over 100 other countries and which the Soviet Union enjoyed until 1951. The issue is whether to abolish discriminatory trade restrictions that were imposed at the height of the Cold War. Indeed, at that time the Soviet Government discouraged commerce because it feared the domestic impact of normal trading relations with the West on its society.

The demand that Moscow modify its domestic policy as a precondition for MFN or détente was never made while we were negotiating; now it is inserted after both sides have carefully shaped an overall mosaic. Thus it raises questions about our entire bilateral relationship.

Finally, the issue affects not only our relationship with the Soviet Union, but also with many other countries whose internal structures we find incompatible with our own. Conditions imposed on one country could inhibit expanding relations with others, such as the People's Republic of China.

We shall never condone the suppression of fundamental liberties. We shall urge humane principles and use our influence to promote justice. But the issue comes down to the limits of such efforts. How hard can we press without provoking the Soviet leadership into returning to practices in its foreign policy that increase international tensions? Are we ready to face the crises and increased defense budgets that a return to Cold War conditions would spawn? And will this encourage full emigration or enhance the well-being or nourish the hope for liberty of the peoples of Eastern Europe and the Soviet Union? Is it détente that has prompted repression—or is it détente that has generated the ferment and the demand for openness which we are now witnessing?

For half a century we have objected to communist efforts to alter the domestic structures of other countries. For a generation of Cold War we sought to ease the risks produced by competing ideologies. Are we now to come full circle and *insist* on domestic compatibility as a condition of progress?

These questions have no easy answers. The government may underestimate the margin of concessions available to us. But a fair debate must admit that they *are* genuine questions, the answers to which could affect the fate of all of us.

Our policy with respect to détente is clear: We shall resist aggressive foreign policies. Détente cannot survive irresponsibility in any area, including the Middle East. As for the internal policies of closed systems, the United States will never forget that the antagonism between freedom and its enemies is part of the reality of the modern age. We are not neutral in that struggle. As long as we remain powerful we will use our influence to promote freedom, as we always have. But in the nuclear age we are obliged to recognize that the issue of war and peace also involves human lives and that the attainment of peace is a profound moral concern.

Addressing the United Nations General Assembly two weeks ago, I described our goal as a world where power blocs and balances are no longer relevant; where justice, not stability, can be our overriding preoccupation; where countries consider cooperation in the world interest to be in their national interest.

But we cannot move toward the world of the future without first maintaining peace in the world as it is. These very days we are vividly reminded that this requires vigilance and a continuing commitment.

So our journey must start from where we are now. This is a time of lessened tension, of greater equilibrium, of diffused power. But if the world is better than our earlier fears, it still falls far short of our hopes. To deal with the present does not mean that we are content with it.

The most striking feature of the contemporary period—the feature that gives complexity as well as hope—is the radical transformation in the nature of power. Throughout history power has generally been homogeneous. Military, economic and political potential were closely related. To be powerful a nation had to be strong in all categories. Today, the vocabulary of strength is more complex. Military muscle does not guarantee political influence. Economic giants can be militarily weak, and military strength may not be able to obscure economic weakness. Countries can exert political influence even when they have neither military nor economic strength.

It is wrong to speak of only one balance of power, for there are several which have to be related to each other. In the military sphere, there are two superpowers. In economic terms, there are at least five major groupings. Politically, many more centers of influence have emerged; some 80 new nations have come into being since the end of World War II and regional groups are assuming ever increasing importance.

Above all, whatever the measure of power, its political utility has changed. Throughout history, increases in military power—however slight—could be turned into specific political advantage. With the overwhelming arsenals of the nuclear age, however, the pursuit of marginal advantage is both pointless and potentially suicidal. Once sufficiency is reached, additional increments of power do not translate into usable political strength; and attempts to achieve tactical gains can lead to cataclysm.

This environment both puts a premium on stability and makes it difficult to maintain. Today's striving for equilibrium should not be compared to the balance of power of previous periods. The very notion of "operating" a classical balance of power disintegrates when the change required to upset the balance is so large that it cannot be achieved by limited means.

More specifically, there is no parallel with the nineteenth century. Then, the principal countries shared essentially similar concepts of legitimacy and accepted the basic structure of the existing international order. Small adjustments in strength were significant. The "balance" operated in a relatively confined geographic area. None of these factors obtains today.

Nor when we talk of equilibrium do we mean a simplistic mechanical model devoid of purpose. The constantly shifting alliances that maintained equilibrium in previous centuries are neither appropriate nor possible in our time. In an age of ideological schism the distinction between friends and adversaries is an objective reality. We share ideals as well as interests with our friends, and we know that the strength of our friendships is crucial to the lowering of tensions with our opponents.

When we refer to five or six or seven major centers of power, the point being made is not that others are excluded but that a few short years ago everyone agreed that there were only two. The diminishing tensions and the emergence of new centers of power has meant greater freedom of action and greater importance for all other nations.

In this setting, our immediate aim has been to build a stable network of relationships that offers hope of sparing mankind the scourges of war. An interdependent world community cannot tolerate either big power confrontations or recurrent regional crises.

But peace must be more than the absence of conflict. We perceive stability as the bridge to the realization of human aspirations, not an end in itself. We have learned much about containing crises, but we have not removed their roots. We have begun to accommodate our differences, but we have not affirmed our commonality. We may have improved the mastery of equilibrium, but we have not yet attained justice.

In the encyclical for which this conference is named, Pope John sketched a greater vision. He foresaw "that no political community is able to pursue its own interests and develop itself in isolation" for "there is a growing awareness of all human beings that they are members of a world community."

The opportunities of mankind now transcend nationalism, and can only be dealt with by nations acting in concert.

— For the first time in generations mankind is in a position to shape a new and peaceful international order. But do we have the imagination and determination to carry forward this still fragile task of creation?

— For the first time in history we may have the technical knowledge to satisfy man's basic needs. The imperatives of the modern world respect no national borders and must inevitably open all societies to the world around them. But do we have the political will to join together to accomplish this great end?

If this vision is to be realized, America's active involvement is inescapable. History will judge us by our deeds, not by our good intentions.

But it cannot be the work of any one country. And it cannot be the undertaking of any one Administration or one branch of government or one party. To build truly is to chart a course that will be carried on by future leaders because it has the enduring support of the American people.

So let us search for a fresh consensus. Let us restore a spirit of understanding between the legislative and the executive, between the government and the press, between the people and their public servants. Let us learn once again to debate our methods and not our motives, to focus on our destiny and not on our divisions. Let us all contribute our different views and perspectives but let us, once again, see ourselves as engaged in a common enterprise. If we are to shape a world community we must first restore community at home.

With Americans working together, America can work with others toward man's eternal goal of a *Pacem in Terris*—peace abroad, peace at home and peace within ourselves.

Henry A. Kissinger is Secretary of State and National Security Adviser to President Richard M. Nixon.

Basic Aspects of the National Interest

J. William Fulbright

One of my themes tonight—unexpectedly more topical than I had expected—is the need for a world rule of law. Regardless of the outcome of the current fighting in Sinai and the Golan Heights, Arabs and Israelis alike are catching a glimpse of their destiny in a world without law. It is a destiny of recurrent war, unending tensions, fear and hate, and a crushing burden of arms. For the fourth time in a generation these otherwise gifted peoples have failed the promise of their own ancient civilizations and plunged into futile hostilities. The failure, however, like the danger, is not theirs alone, but that of the entire civilized world, which solemnly committed itself at San Francisco in 1945 "to save succeeding generations from the scourge of war, which twice in our lifetime has brought untold sorrow to mankind . . ."

It is possible, though hardly likely, that the Arabs and Israelis are content to continue the struggle, each in vain hope of some ultimate victory. I cannot believe that really is their wish because of the enormous costs to themselves and the bleakness of the future which continuing struggle will bring. The Arab states, including those which are now conservative, are likely to be radicalized as their grievances fester. Israel, already a garrison state, faces the prospect of mounting terrorism and recurrent war, of a national existence with no semblance of security. However confident they may be of their own military prowess, the Israelis can hardly relish this prospect.

But even if the combatants can accept the prospect of unending struggle, the outside world cannot. As long as there is danger of other nations being drawn in—and that danger is constant—the world cannot stand aside. Like the Balkans in 1914, the Middle East has become the potential flash point of world conflict. In addition, there is the energy problem. Call it what you like—blackmail or ordinary business—the Arab Middle East possesses at least 300 billion of the 500 billion barrels of proven world oil reserves. With no spare productive capacity of its own, the United States—like other industrial nations—is increasingly dependent on Middle Eastern oil, and consequently in need of good relations with the producing countries. These countries, it is well to remember, have no direct quarrel with the United States and have never done anything to harm the United States. Our dependence on their oil is a matter of national interest, no more so perhaps than our emotional bond to Israel, but surely no less so either. These are matters which affect all nations, and because they go beyond the Arab-Israeli conflict itself, the outside world has the right and responsibility to participate in the making of a settlement.

The first requirement is an immediate cease-fire—not a delayed cease-fire which might allow one side or the other to impose "new facts," but an immediate cease-fire ordered by the United Nations Security Council in accordance with its authority under Chapter VII of the Charter, to "decide what measures shall be taken" to restore peace. Beyond a cease-fire, the Security Council ought now, without delay and with full support from the U.S., to implement its resolution of November 22

1967, by persuasion if possible, by enforcement if necessary, in accordance with the terms of the United Nations Charter. That resolution, officially supported by the United States through the "Rogers Plan" of 1969, calls for the withdrawal of Israeli forces from the occupied territories, but also provides for Israel's survival and security by requiring the "termination of all claims of states or belligerency and respect for and acknowledgment of the sovereignty, territorial integrity and political independence of every state in the area."

Given a will to settle, reasonable variations on the Security Council resolution of November, 1967 might be worked out to bolster Israel's security. The Rogers Plan allows "insubstantial alterations" of territory for the sake of mutual security, and these could include the retention by Israel of some part of the Golan Heights from which the Syrians, before 1967, fired down upon civilian communities. In addition, arrangements might be made for the phased restoration of Sinai by Egypt along with a general acknowledgment of Egypt's sovereignty over the region. Israel's right of free access through the Gulf of Aqaba might be secured by the stationing at Sharm el Sheikh of an international force, removable only by the consent of all parties, or alternately by an Israeli leasehold comparable to the special French presence in the German Saar after the first world war.

Jerusalem, because of its profound importance to three great religions, can and should be made an international city. Its sacredness to Jews is well-known, but its equal importance to Muslims has not been fully appreciated in the West. It may be recalled that in 1967, by a vote of 99 to 0 in which the United States abstained, the United Nations General Assembly condemned Israel's unilateral annexation of the city. Its status now cannot be accepted as "non-negotiable."

All these arrangements could be guaranteed by a binding arrangement, duly ratified, between Israel, the Arab states and the United Nations. In addition—as I have suggested on several previous occasions—a United Nations guarantee could be supplemented by an identical bilateral treaty between Israel and the United States—not an executive agreement but a treaty consented to by the Senate—under which the United States would guarantee the territory and independence of Israel within its adjusted borders. This supplementary, bilateral arrangement with Israel would obligate the United States to use force if necessary, in accordance with its constitutional processes, to assist Israel against any violation of its borders which it could not repel itself, but the agreement would also obligate Israel, firmly and unequivocally, never to violate those borders herself.

The conflict in the Middle East is testimony to the bankruptcy of traditional power politics. Had the nations met their responsibilities under the United Nations Charter in 1948 or 1956 or 1967, any or all of these three wars could have been avoided. Now, once again, tragedy brings opportunity. As will be shown in the remarks which follow, I am less than confident of the rational and humane conduct of human affairs. But neither have I given up on that possibility. I perceive in the Middle East a unique opportunity to make the United Nations work as it was intended to work, and by doing so, not only to resolve the conflict between Arabs and Israelis, but also to create a most valuable precedent for the future.

Perhaps in the abstract sense there is an objective category which can be called the national interest. Human affairs, however, are not conducted in the abstract, and as one moves from the theoretical to the operational, objectivity diminishes and sentiment rises; ideas give way to ideology, principle to personality, reasons to rationalization. As formulated by men of power, the national interest is a subjective and even capricious potpourri, with ingredients of strategic advantage, economic aspiration, national pride, group emotion, and the personal vanity of the leaders themselves. This is not to suggest that the concept of national interest is false but that it is elusive and far from self-evident, and when statesmen invoke it, they raise more questions than they answer.

There have been in recent American usage at least three separate conceptions of national interest: the ideological, exemplified by the anti-communist crusade of the Cold War; the geopolitical, which treats international relations as an endless struggle for power as an end in itself; and the legal-institutional, an approach which holds that international affairs, like domestic affairs, must be brought under the regulation of law, an approach which gave rise, under American leadership, to the League of Nations Covenant and the United Nations Charter. Depending upon which approach you embrace, or deplore, your conception of the national interest will vary from, or conflict with, another. My own preference—bias, if you like—is toward the legal-institutional. The preference of the Nixon Administration, as I perceive it, is strongly geopolitical. Though divergent in concept, these approaches often overlap in practice; I find myself, for instance, in agreement with the Administration on the wisdom of détente with the Soviet Union, but in disagreement on certain underlying concepts of what the national interest is and what it is not.

It is not my intention here to offer a definitive catalogue of the national interests of the United States, but rather to comment on certain aspects of the national interest which I believe to be illustrative of its basic character. I shall not comment on the emergence of China as a leading and accepted nation, except to take note of the extraordinary experiment in social cooperation within China which may well prove exemplary for much of the third world, and also to express hope that China will play a leading and responsible role in strengthening the United Nations. Nor do I comment here on the seemingly intractable problems of poverty and population growth in the third world. In all of these the United States has major national interests, but I confine myself here to a discussion of basic concepts of national interest, of the fragile and threatened détente with the Soviet Union, of the need to restore economic health at home, and the continuing significance of the all-but-forgotten promise of the United Nations. Though by no means definitive, these areas seem to me to be both topical and illustrative of the kinds of national policy which are consistent with our national tradition, congenial to our national character, and best conceived, overall, to advance the security and welfare of the American people.

It has ceased to be useful, if ever it was, to deal with foreign policy as a category distinct from domestic policy. Neither can be rationally conceived or successfully executed except as aspects of *national* policy. I am thinking not of the policy-maker's natural preference for strong domestic support of his foreign policy, but of the more fundamental need of a foreign policy which advances the well-being of our people, does not drain resources unduly, and is compatible with the national character. In the course of history, nations have been defeated by foreign enemies at least as often because of the internal weaknesses of their societies as because of insufficient armaments. But I would go even beyond the fact of demonstrable interaction between foreign and domestic problems to suggest that a well-conceived foreign policy is not only related to, but necessarily subordinate to, domestic needs and aspirations. In 1969, a report to the Senate Foreign Relations Committee on "National Commitments" noted, "Foreign policy is not an end in itself. We do not have a foreign policy because it is interesting or fun, or because it satisfies some basic human need; we conduct foreign policy for a purpose external to itself, the purpose of securing democratic values in our own country." To put the matter simply:

our national interest has to do with the kind of society we live in, and only incidentally with the kinds of society other people live in.

It is mistaken to conceive of foreign policy as an adventure, even an idealistic adventure. Echoing General de Gaulle's mystical conception of France's role, Secretary Kissinger has suggested twice recently that "America was not true to itself unless it had a meaning beyond itself"—a "spiritual" meaning, he went on to explain. Secretary Kissinger, during his confirmation hearings before the Senate Foreign Relations Committee, also endorsed Theodore Roosevelt's entreaty that we "dare mighty things" and "win glorious triumphs." That invocation, the Secretary said, "epitomizes the essence and strength of this nation." I do not know exactly what "mighty things" to be dared the Secretary of State has in mind, but I must say that I find the notion disturbing. It is my impression that Theodore Roosevelt was an impetuous and enthusiastic chauvinist with imperialistic tendencies. There may have been a kind of romantic idealism in his outlook, but it is the wrong kind of idealism, dangerous and obsolete in this nuclear age.

Foreign policy is not an adventure, and our statesmen are not cavaliers but public servants. It is not daring but competence and prudence that are required of them. When they forget that, and take flight with their own soaring rhetoric, they get into trouble, and drag the rest of us with them. I do not agree with Secretary Kissinger that our American experience necessarily has "universal meaning," or that America requires a meaning beyond itself. There is meaning enough in being ourselves, a meaning by no means yet fulfilled, and in letting others find their own meanings.

The primacy of domestic policy has nothing to do with "isolationism"—a concept which has become functionally irrelevant as well as rhetorically polemical. The charge of "neo-isolationism" is an invention of people who confuse internationalism with an intrusive American interventionism, with a quasi-imperialism. Those of us who are called "neo-isolationists" are, I believe, the opposite: internationalists in the classical sense of the term, in the sense in which it was brought into American usage by Woodrow Wilson and Franklin Roosevelt. We believe in international cooperation through international institutions. We would like to try to keep the peace through the United Nations, and we would like to try to assist the poor countries through such institutions as the World Bank. We do not think the United Nations is a failure; we think it has never been tried.

The merit of the Nixon-Kissinger foreign policy is that it is rooted in a coherent view of the world; the principal failing of the Nixon-Kissinger policy is the particular world-view in which it is rooted. The power politics approach is an improvement on the ideological crusade of the Cold War, and the Administration deserves credit for the openings to China and Russia which have alleviated the Cold War. But the balance-of-power approach, on which our new relationships with China and Russia are based, is justly criticized as cold and amoral, oriented to process rather than purpose, as if the "game" of nations were nothing but a game, conducted for the sake of the game, not for winning *something*, but just for the sake of winning, for being "number one." But the ultimate failing of supposedly hard-headed, realistic power politics is that, always in the long-run and often in the short-run as well, the approach turns out to be neither hard-headed nor realistic as a means of keeping the peace. However successful the balance-of-power approach has been in keeping the peace over certain periods of time, it has always broken down in the end, culminating, as in 1914, in general war.

There are many reasons for the inherent instability of power politics. One is the failure to take account of the internal life of nations. In the eighteenth century, the kings of Europe were able to alter and adjust the balance of power through shifting alliances; even in 1939 the Hitler-Stalin pact shattered the last remaining fragment of European stability. For the most part, however, modern nations gain and lose strength, and with it the ability to upset the international equilibrium, as the result of internal developments. Germany upset the European balance in the late nineteenth century primarily because her economy and industry grew much faster than those of her neighbors, enabling Germany to become militarily preponderant. More recently, France has reclaimed a leading role in Europe despite the loss of empire, more accurately perhaps *because* of it; the stability of the Fifth Republic and the rapid growth of the French economy since the Algerian war have given France a new weight in international affairs. Conversely, and more pertinently, we have seen the influence and reputation of the United States in world affairs diminished by political scandal and economic dislocations, the latter largely the result of extravagant military spending. Confrontations, summits, alliances and spheres-of-influence are surely factors in a nation's position in the world, but they are no longer the major factors; the major factors are internal.

A skillful diplomacy can, of course, take account of domestic developments, but here we are thrown back upon the cleverness of statesmen—a commodity hardly to be relied upon. And that indeed is *the root weakness of the game of nations:* it is a despotism without laws, as stable or shaky, just or unjust, as the men momentarily at the top of the heap. In international relations, as within our own country, stability requires institutions; it requires a system that *ordinary* men can run and incompetent men cannot ruin. Guarantee if you can that the game will be played by a Bismarck or Talleyrand, by a Kissinger or Le Duc Tho, and perhaps I will withdraw my objections. But as long as luminaries give way to lesser lights—and they always do—the objection stands. As

Henry Kissinger once wrote of Prince Bismarck, "In the hands of others lacking his subtle touch, his methods led to the collapse of the nineteenth century state system. The nemesis of power is that, except in the hands of a master, reliance on it is more likely to produce a contest of arms than of self-restraint."

That brings me to the nub of both my concurrence with, and dissent from, the Nixon-Kissinger foreign policy. I concur, strongly, in the efforts toward a "structure of peace," but I am concerned with the flimsiness of the structure. It is makeshift and fragile, too dependent on agility and cleverness, too delicate to work for dull leaders or withstand incompetent ones. I remain, therefore, a Wilsonian, a seeker still of a world system of laws rather than of men, a believer still in the one great new idea of this century in the field of international relations, the idea of an international organization with permanent processes for the peaceful settlement of international disputes.

Reluctant though we may be to relate foreign policy to our domestic affairs, we seem all too willing at times to apply our foreign policy to other people's domestic affairs. The Jackson amendment to the trade bill pending in Congress would deny most-favored-nation trade treatment to the Soviet Union—which is to say discriminate against its trade—unless the Soviet Union eliminates restrictions on emigration by its citizens. On September 17, 1973, the Senate, on the initiative of Senator Walter Mondale, adopted a resolution, without referral to a committee and with minimum discussion, asking the President to press the Soviet Government to stop oppressing dissidents and permit its citizens freedom of expression and emigration. Under the Mondale resolution the President is called upon to negotiate nothing less than a revamping of the Soviet system, and the dismantling of a police state apparatus going back half a century under the communists, and a thousand years before that under the tsars. It is a worthy sentiment but a tall order.

Nonintervention in internal affairs of other countries is one of the cardinal rules of international law and relations, and it is codified in the United Nations Charter. The essential purpose of the rule of nonintervention is to prevent larger countries from bullying smaller ones, and to prevent quarrels arising from gratuitous meddling. There are times when nonintervention seems harsh and immoral, as when an oppressive government is left free to mistreat its own people. At times an exception may be warranted, as when a society disintegrates into barbarism, or when an internal issue becomes a threat to international peace, as that is defined in the United Nations Charter. *Much more often than not, however, nonintervention is more likely to advance justice than to detract from it.* As we Americans discovered in Vietnam, outsiders are seldom wise enough, just enough, or disinterested enough to advance the morality or welfare of a society not their own. The Russian people have lived under dictatorship throughout their history; it is not for us, at this late date, to try to change that by external pressure, especially at a time when there is a better chance than ever to build a cooperative relationship between the Soviet Union and the United States.

Why indeed should we cooperate with the Soviet Union, a country whose social system is inimical to our own? The answer is simplicity itself: we have to get along with the Russians because, in matters of world peace, we cannot get along without them. The threat of nuclear destruction has become commonplace, so much so that we tend to dismiss it. But the fact remains that the leaders of the two nations have the means at their disposal at any time to destroy each other's cities and much or most of each other's populations, and there is nothing—*nothing*—either side could do to prevent it. American pioneer families helped each other to build cabins and clear the land because the job was too big to do alone—cooperation was a matter of survival. Similarly, the Bedouin Arabs have an ancient etiquette of hospitality—a traveller across the desert cannot be refused food and water, because the host knows that he too may someday journey across the desert. Here too it is a matter of survival—not of affection or friendship or religion or ideology. That is the sum and substance of it: in matters of war and peace Russians and Americans are wanderers in the same desert, and in that desert it is not ideology that counts but food and water—the "food and water" of trade, arms control, political cooperation and cultural exchange.

For this essential reason, while I sympathize with the plight of the dissident intellectuals and minorities in the Soviet Union, I cannot concur in the approach of Andrei Sakharov, the Soviet physicist, who says that there can be no détente without democracy, or the novelist Aleksandr Solzhenitsyn, who says that "man-kind's sole salvation lies in everyone making everything his business." This asks too much of human nature, assuming that involvement will always be benign rather than aggressive, moral rather than predatory. Were everyone to make everything his business, the result would be war, not peace, imperialism, not democracy. Men have capricious notions of what is and is not their business; that is why it is usually better for them to mind their own. I do believe that the world can be made better, and that man is capable of aiding its betterment, but I am equally a believer in selectivity of means. Important as it is to know what we hope to achieve, it is equally important to know what we are incapable of achieving; which is to say that humane aspiration must be tempered by realism.

Selectivity is inevitable in politics, even on the part of those who would base détente upon sweeping standards of morality. Why indeed are we distressed by the denial of civil rights in the Soviet Union, when we have amicable relations with a large number of non-communist dictatorships? Why do we suddenly require measures of democracy in the Soviet Union as the price of our trade? In Chile a freely-elected but Marxist government has been overthrown by a book-burning military dictatorship; will we require a return to democracy before resuming trade and investment? If we wish to apply pressure for democracy and human rights, would it not make sense to start with Chile, Brazil or Greece, all of whom are vulnerable to American pressures, none of whom are essential partners for the maintenance of world peace? Why start with the Soviet Union, a superpower which can, if it must, live without our trade and investment, and the one country whose cooperation is absolutely essential for building a structure of peace?

The adoption of the Jackson amendment, requiring continued discrimination against Soviet trade, may not in itself destroy the détente between the Soviet Union and the United States, *but it may well derail it.* We may recall that in 1960 the U-2 affair shattered the Eisenhower-Khrushchev "spirit of Camp David," and that the Cuban missile crisis precipitated a renewal of the arms race. Khrushchev went on to conclude the partial nuclear test ban treaty with President Kennedy, but his position at home had been irreparably weakened by his failures in attempting to get along with the Americans, and he was displaced in 1964.

Party chief Leonid Brezhnev has now reiterated Khrushchev's request for businesslike dealings with the United States. In Moscow last year, significant agreements were reached in the field of arms control—especially the ABM treaty—and for cooperation in such fields as space, science and health. Now the Russians are interested primarily in trade and investment, and, without being gullible or naive, surely we owe it to ourselves to give openminded consideration to Mr. Brezhnev's assurance to members of Congress, "We came here to consolidate good things, not to quarrel." If Brezhnev, like Khrushchev, fails in his détente policy because of American pressures on emigration and the treatment of Soviet intellectuals, it is possible that Brezhnev, like Khrushchev, will be discredited at home and displaced by hard-nosed successors who will have little interest in trade, arms control or détente with the United States, or in freedom of thought or emigration for Soviet citizens.

The Soviet Government, it is true, has already yielded a great deal under our pressure: emigration to Israel, which was kept to only 1,000 three years ago, is now being permitted at a rate of over 30,000 a year. But we should not conclude that the Russians will continue indefinitely to yield to American pressure. The adoption of the Jackson amendment might induce the Russians to remove remaining restraints, or it might anger them into clamping the controls back on. If ever there is to be authentic liberalization in the Soviet Union, it will come about as a result of internal pressures from increasingly assertive professional, managerial and intellectual elements within the Soviet Union.

Like the tsars before them, the Soviet leaders greatly fear Western political ideas, which they consider a threat to their rule. It is understandable, though not admirable, that they should tighten internal controls at the same time that they are seeking closer political and economic ties with the West. They fear our subversion, just as we once feared theirs; specifically, they fear that we will try to bring our political ideas into their country along with the trade and investment which they desire. The Jackson amendment reinforces these fears and, in so doing, threatens the political and economic cooperation which both sides need and desire.

I would judge that the most we can do to advance the cause of liberties within the Soviet Union is to help create an international atmosphere of security and cordiality, an atmosphere calculated to diminish rather than aggravate neurotic fears of Western ideas on the part of the Soviet leaders. In practice this would mean a continuation of measures of détente already begun, in trade, investment, cultural exchange, and above all arms control.

While recognizing the futility of war, the super-powers refuse to recognize the resulting futility of their arms race. Instead of pursuing the logic of the ABM treaty and proceeding energetically with the SALT talks, they prepare for future agreements by feverishly accumulating "bargaining chips," which is to say, by arming to the teeth. To cite one recent example: on September 27, 1973, the Senate by a narrow margin voted $1.6 billion to allow the Administration to *accelerate* the development of Trident, a new class of submarines, carrying strategic nuclear weapons. Each single Trident submarine will cost an estimated $1.3 billion, and that does not allow for the Pentagon's inevitable cost-overruns. The decision to accelerate the Trident program was made in the wake of the 1972 "interim agreement," so as to give the United States additional "bargaining chips" in the negotiations for a permanent treaty, and despite the fact that our Polaris and Poseidon submarines, equipped with nuclear missiles, are virtually invulnerable to attack, and likely to remain so for the foreseeable future. As former U. N. Ambassador Charles Yost has written, "When Congress votes funds for a submarine it votes not for one but for two, an American and a Soviet." Progress toward arms control—the most important single area of Soviet-American détente—is thus negated by the self-defeating theory of "bargaining chips." If we are to have the "structure of peace" of which President Nixon and Secretary Kissinger speak, it is essential that we terminate this irrational, ruinously costly practice of accelerating the arms race while trying to restrict it.

Until and unless China joins the other great powers in their ill-considered arms race, her significance will consist primarily in the challenge of her society. Visitors to China—experts and amateurs alike—report on the orderliness, purposefulness, cleanliness, and cooperativeness of Chinese society. Perhaps, to some degree, they have been misled by guided tours; perhaps their reports reflect something of the old condescending sentimentalism of Americans toward China. The evidence suggests, however, that there is more to the modern Chinese experiment. The evidence suggests that this largest of human communities and oldest of civilizations has moved far to bring health, education, social cohesion and a sense of purpose into the lives of a long-divided, poverty-stricken and demoralized population.

The world significance of the Chinese experiment is its potential impact on the third world. China alone of the great powers has a claim to membership in the third world. As an economically less-developed nation itself, China has the potentiality of serving as the model for Asian, African, and Latin American nations to whom the experience of economically developed nations like the Soviet Union and the United States may seem irrelevant. It seems possible, therefore, that neither of the missile-wielding superpowers will prevail in the competition for influence in the third world, but that the role of an exemplar will fall to China as one of their own. It is in this respect—not as a "power" but as a society—that China commands a position of primacy in our foreign policy and in our national interest, warranting our attention, our friendly interest and our best efforts toward understanding. Secretary Kissinger commented after his visit to China in early 1972, "These people have a sense of purpose. If there is communication, it will be a great challenge to our whole society."

If détente with the Soviet Union and with China represents the first foreign requirement in the national interest, the first requirement on the domestic side is the restoration of a healthy national economy. The two, as we have seen, are inseparable: extravagant military expenditures strain our economy, and the weakened economy in turn detracts from our foreign policy. The essential corrective is a more restrained American role in world affairs, a reduction in status, so to speak, from "number one" to something like "first among equals."

On August 15, 1971, the day President Nixon imposed emergency controls on the economy, the United States passed through a symbolic watershed in its foreign policy. Prior to that date we had felt ourselves able to shape our foreign policy solely in terms of what we needed and wished to accomplish in the world. Since that time we have been compelled—or should have been compelled—to recognize that our resources are limited and that we must base our policy decisions not only on what we wish to do but also on what we can afford.

Some cogent statistics illustrate the change. In 1950, the United States produced half of the world's total output of goods and services; by 1970, our share had dropped to 30 per cent. In 1950, we produced almost half of the world's steel; today, we produce about one-fifth. In 1950, the United States held half of the world's monetary reserves; today, we hold less than one-tenth.

The significance of these developments, by no means yet fully appreciated, is that the United States can no longer afford, and no longer can fairly be expected, to sustain the military and political supervision of world affairs which it has exercised for three decades. The role of global colossus came to us by default after World War II when every other major industrial nation in the world was economically devastated. We thereupon undertook extraordinary global—and even extra-global—enterprises, including the Marshall Plan, the rearmament of ourselves and our allies, worldwide military and economic aid programs, two long and costly wars, the extravagantly expensive arms race with the Soviet Union and a superheated race to the moon.

Only recently, with our national economy beginning to crack under the strain, have we been constrained to recognize the necessity of bringing our military and political activities back into harmony with their economic base. For this purpose economic controls are only temporary expedients. They are no substitute for the fiscal and monetary reforms which are essential to curb inflation, stem the dollar outflow, and restore confidence at home and abroad in the American economy and its managers. However many "phases" of control and de-control are superimposed on our national economy, a stable equilibrium can be restored only through some combination of increased revenues and reduced expenditures.

The most promising field by far for reducing expenditures without risk to our national security is in the development of unessential new weapons systems. A Brookings Institution economist, Edward R. Fried, suggests that savings of $10 billion could be made without appreciably altering current military capabilities by major economies in the use of manpower and by slowing down the development of such weapons systems as the Trident submarine and the B-1 supersonic bomber, the one designed to supplant the still-functional Polaris, the other to supplant the still quite adequate B-52 bomber. There are, in addition, numerous military aid projects, troop deployments, and other foreign operations which, though individually modest in cost, are quite costly in the aggregate and of dubious relevance, in any case, to the national interest.

In practice if not in their declarations, Congress and the Nixon Administration reject the concept of interacting foreign and domestic policies. Congress pays eloquent tribute to the need for economy but votes just about everything the Administration requests for arms procurement; the Senate declined last week to cut even $500 million from a whopping $20.9 billion arms procurement bill. The Nixon Administration, for its part, pursues détente with the Soviet Union, but at the same time pursues an arms policy which goes against détente and which strains our national economy. *The defense budget for the fiscal year 1974 is still based on outdated Cold War assumptions and on the equally outdated assumption of unlimited American resources to prosecute it.* Conceived, as it seems, in isolated compartments, the overall

Administration policy is one of pressing the Cold War while also trying to end it, of straining the national economy while also trying to revive it.

Karl Marx predicted that the capitalist countries would ultimately collapse under the weight of their own internal contradictions. Our current ambivalence as between détente and Cold War, extravagant weapons systems and the needs of the domestic economy, lend more than an iota of credibility to the Marxian prophecy. On the one side Senators and Congressmen sincerely advocate détente; on the other they vote for expensive and unnecessary weapons systems. On the one side the President and Congress take statesmen's advice on the possibilities of international accommodation; on the other side they accept the generals' drastic estimates of a possible adversary's capacity and intentions. The effects of these contradictions are self-defeating abroad and debilitating at home.

Lord Salisbury, a British Prime Minister of the late nineteenth century, said to a colleague, "You listen too much to the soldiers ... you should never trust the experts. If you believe the doctors, nothing is wholesome; if you believe the theologians, nothing is innocent; if you believe the soldiers, nothing is safe." We are in need of an overview, one which will put risks and costs, projects and opportunities in clarifying perspective.

Shortly before he entered government, Secretary Kissinger wrote that "The greatest need of the contemporary international system is an agreed concept of order." I surely do agree that a concept of order is essential to the world and essential to our own national interest. I agree too that the Nixon Administration's foreign policy has had a more well-defined central concept than that of any Administration since Woodrow Wilson's. But, as noted before, I believe the Nixon concept to be inadequate, reactionary in the historical sense, and profoundly pessimistic; reconciled as it is to struggle for power as something permanent and inevitable, the Nixon-Kissinger approach is essentially devoid of hope for progress or betterment in human affairs. Believing as I do that there is hope, however slight, for fundamental change and fundamental improvement in the way nations deal with one another, I retain my faith in the Wilsonian concept of a powerful world peace-keeping organization, not really because I am confident of its coming about or of its success, but because I think it is within the range of human possibility to make a world organization work, and that seems worth striving for.

It follows from this conception of the national interest that the United Nations ought to be at the very center of our foreign policy and not at its far periphery. In this connection, I was disappointed by the lack of conviction and detail in Secretary Kissinger's recent speech to the United Nations, and by his "unnecessarily modest proposals"—as *The New York Times* put it—for strengthening the world organization.

The United Nations—despised, neglected and misused—remains nonetheless the greatest potential instrument for dealing with the global problems of our time. When all is said and done—when all the ideologies have been exposited and found wanting, when all the theories of *realpolitik* have been tested and revealed as dangerous romanticisms—one ancient, still untested idea persists: the idea that politics can be put to the service of ordinary human needs; the idea that through world law we can free ourselves from the costly and dangerous burden of international conflict; the idea that through cooperation and man's genius we can alleviate poverty and put our technology to humane and rational purposes. It is the age-old dream of beating swords into plowshares, of changing the rules of the old, discredited game by supplanting the anarchy of nations with an effective international organization.

To begin to achieve these great aims, we must recognize that the principle of absolute national sovereignty is obsolete. We must begin to think of the world as a community in which, for certain limited purposes at least, the good of the whole must take precedence over the advantage of the parts. Neither the large countries, including our own, nor the small countries have ever accepted that principle with respect to the United Nations. The large nations, including the United States, have used the United Nations as a minor instrument of their own foreign policies, to be used or—more commonly—ignored according to their convenience.

The United States is only just turning away from a long period of unilateralism, in the course of which we allowed ourselves to believe that we ourselves were the effective successors to an enfeebled United Nations, forced by fate and circumstance to bear the "responsibilities of power." In so doing we not only went beyond our own legitimate interests and responsibilities, we discouraged others from accepting their fair share of international responsibility. Unilateralism fed upon itself: having gotten in the habit of acting on our own because others seemed unwilling to act, we then found them more unwilling than ever to accept collective responsibilities. For this reason, and for the even more important reason that long-neglected domestic needs now claim our attention, the United States can make a great contribution to international cooperation by making it clear that the *Pax Americana*—such as it has been—is now at an end, and that hereafter the United States will act promptly and loyally in concert with other nations in the United Nations but will not act alone.

Even without the immediate cooperation of others, there is much the United States could do to breathe life into the United Nations. We could make it national policy to appoint men or women of eminence and power—of the caliber of the late Governor Adlai Stevenson or the late Senator Robert Taft—as our representatives in the United Nations. We could make it national policy to refrain from using our veto in the Security Council. We could make it known to other great powers that the United Nations is our preferred forum for negotiations on arms control and other crucial issues. And we could take the lead in negotiating those long-neglected agreements called for by Article 43 of the Charter, under which members would "make available to the Security Council . . . armed forces, assistance and facilities" to deal with threats to and breaches of the peace.

We have survived in the nuclear age so far not through any "agreed concept of order," but through crisis diplomacy and that frail substitute for a "concept of order" known as the balance of power. At its best the old system was only fairly successful in preventing and limiting war, but in the age of nuclear weapons only one breakdown would result in catastrophe, quite possibly in the destruction of civilized human life in much of the world. Sooner or later the law of averages is going to run out on us.

There is very little in international affairs about which I feel certain but there is one thing of which I am quite certain: the necessity of fundamental change in the way nations conduct their relations with each other. There is nothing in the human environment, as Adlai Stevenson once reminded us, to prevent us from bringing about such fundamental change. The obstacles are within us, in the workings of the human mind. But just as it is the source of so many of our troubles, the inventive mind of man is sometimes capable of breaking through barriers of prejudice and ancient attitude. In the field of international affairs, I believe, such a breakthrough was achieved with the formation, first, of the Covenant of the League of Nations, then of the United Nations Charter. The next breakthrough, urgently awaited, is to make the conception work.

Senator J. William Fulbright of Arkansas is Chairman of the Senate Foreign Relations Committee.

Détente and Human Rights

Henry M. Jackson

At no time since the end of World War II has the Western democratic world been more hopeful, nor the struggling democrats in the East more apprehensive, at the prospects of the developing international détente. And nowhere should the fears and apprehensions of those whose love of freedom has survived behind the iron curtain find a more receptive and thoughtful consideration than at a gathering devoted to *Pacem in Terris.* My remarks, therefore, are devoted to the question of détente and human rights.

On Monday night, the Secretary of State and the Chairman of the Senate Foreign Relations Committee— who agree on little else—came before you to share their belief that it is wrong for the United States to condition trade concessions to the Soviet Union on adherence to the free emigration provision of the Universal Declaration of Human Rights.

Senator Fulbright, who is beguiled by the Soviets, and Secretary Kissinger, who believes that he is beguiling them, manage to find common ground in rejecting the great Russian physicist Andrei Sakharov's wise counsel against promoting a détente unaccompanied by increased openness and trust.

I believe in the Universal Declaration of Human Rights; and I believe that now, twenty-five years after its adoption by the United Nations, it is not too late or too early to begin to implement it. And I am sustained in the belief that the best way to do this is through pressing my amendment to the trade bill with these brave words from Andrei Sakharov:

> The abandonment of a policy of principle would be a betrayal of the thousands of Jews and non-Jews who want to emigrate, of the hundreds in camps and mental hospitals, of the victims of the Berlin Wall.
>
> Such a denial would lead to stronger repressions on ideological grounds. It would be tantamount to total capitulation of democratic principles in the face of blackmail, deceit and violence. The consequences of such a capitulation for international confidence, détente and the entire future of mankind are difficult to predict.
>
> I express the hope that the Congress of the United States, reflecting the will and the traditional love of freedom of the American people, will realize its historical responsibility before mankind and will find the strength to rise above temporary partisan considerations of commercialism and prestige.
>
> I hope that the Congress will support the Jackson Amendment.

In an age of nuclear weapons, Senator Fulbright suggests, the Soviet Union is "the one country whose cooperation is absolutely essential." Secretary Kissinger, who recognizes that our traditional commitment to individual liberty poses moral dilemmas, implies that this commitment must be weighed against "the profound moral concern . . . the attainment of peace." Senator Fulbright hints darkly that our very survival may depend on the pursuit of a détente without human rights.

But is the risk of nuclear war really going to increase if the Congress conditions most-favored-nation treatment of the Soviet Union on free emigration? Does Senator Fulbright believe that the Soviet Union will be any less cautious about the risks of a suicidal nuclear war if we choose not to subsidize their foreign borrowing? I concur in Sakharov's belief that "the danger of nuclear war continues to be the foremost concern for all of humanity," and with him I support "all measures to avert this danger including proposed measures of armament reduction." The process of reducing the risks of nuclear war can and will continue because it is in the mutual interest of both the United States and the Soviet Union to do so. But the development of more extensive mutual interests, of a closer and more cordial relationship between the two countries, must be based on something more solid and more enduring and more comprehensive than bargain-basement credits and one-sided commercial transactions.

A true peace, an enduring peace, can only be built on a moral consensus. What better place to begin building this consensus than on the principles embodied in the Universal Declaration of Human Rights, among which the right to choose the country one lives in—the right to emigrate freely—is perhaps the most basic?

We are asked to believe that the prospects for peace are enhanced by the flow of Pepsi-Cola to the Soviet Union and the flow of vodka to the United States. I say that we will move much further along the road to a stable peace when we see the free flow of people and ideas across the barriers that divide East from West—a flow unchecked by arbitrary and capricious power.

Now, at this time in history, we have been presented with an unparalleled opportunity. The growth of the Soviet economy—the means by which the Soviet Union has so long been hoping to "overtake and surpass" the United States—has begun to falter badly. The Soviet economy, despite enormous inefficiencies, had managed to sustain significant economic growth only by resort to a staggering rate of capital investments, twice that of the United States. In recent years, the productivity of that capital has declined drastically. The inflexible Soviet economy has found it increasingly difficult to assimilate modern technology. Even massive infusion of their own capital no longer promises to sustain economic growth.

If the Soviet Union were a minor country with no external ambitions, it might stagger along indefinitely with a no-growth or slow-growth economy. But she is not such a country—and therein lies our opportunity and our challenge. The task that the Soviet leaders wish to impose on their rigid economic system is nothing less than to make the Soviet Union the dominant world power— economically, militarily and politically. They hope to achieve a high rate of economic growth and hold their economy up as a model for the less developed world. They want to continue to divert a disproportionate share of their resources to military spending—more than twice the percentage of GNP as in our case—to sustain their build-up of strategic arms and conventional forces in Eastern Europe and on the Chinese border—and to underwrite the military forces of their Arab allies. The Soviet government needs desperately to improve the quality and quantity of goods available to the Soviet consumer, because it is only too aware of the political threat posed by the continued frustration of consumer demands. Yet the Soviet leaders are also afraid—or perhaps they do not know how—to relax their rigidly controlled economy—and so they have come to us for help. We would be ill-advised to treat this request as just another business proposition—or even as a routine request for foreign aid.

In my judgment, the most abundant and positive source of much needed help for the Soviet economy should come, not from the United States, but through a reordering of Soviet priorities away from the military into the civilian sector. And, in this connection, it is high time that we propose serious disarmament at the SALT negotiations and not just arms control—not the sort of fiddling at the margins that has characterized the approach to arms control thus far, but serious reductions of strategic weapons on both sides. I see no reason, for example, why we cannot, in concert with the Soviet Union, agree that 900 ICBMs and 35 submarines carrying strategic nuclear missiles are adequate for both sides. Would this not be better than the present situation in which they have 1,600 ICBMs and are building toward 62 submarines and we have 1,000 ICBMs and 41 submarines?

The Soviets are seeking billions of dollars in U.S. government subsidized credits—long-term loans at six per cent interest. Neither Secretary Kissinger nor Senator Fulbright chose to dwell on this aspect of what the Secretary of State euphemistically termed "a carefully-shaped, overall mosaic." What is involved here are credit transfers that will dwarf last year's grain deal—or, as I prefer to call it, the great grain robbery.

There are, in my judgment, countries and purposes more deserving of our assistance, whose needs are greater—in some cases dire—and whose use of our aid for humanitarian purposes is more readily assured. The drought-stricken nations of interior West Africa come immediately to mind.

Let us not lose this opportunity to bargain hard for human rights. Let us not be misled by arguments that the time is not yet ripe or that we will be able to accomplish more later, after we have enmeshed the Soviets in some entangling web of investments and business deals. As Secretary Kissinger so eloquently stated here a few nights ago, opportunities once lost may never recur again. What are now clearly recognized by the Russians as concessions on our part will eventually be demanded as the normal way of doing things. Already we see Secretary Kissinger insisting that the discretion of the Congress to grant or deny or condition most-favored-nation status no longer exists because he has bargained it away, never minding that he had no authority to do so. Does anyone believe that American corporations will be more willing, when they have massive investments to protect, to insist on the rights of Soviet dissenters than they are now? At this moment we have an opportunity—which may not again be repeated—when the Soviet people are graced with men with the stature and prestige of Sakharov and Solzhenitsyn who have courageously spoken out on behalf of human rights. Their plea must not fall on deaf ears.

As Sakharov said in his open letter to the U.S. Congress:

> The Jackson Amendment is made even more significant by the fact that the world is only just entering on a new course of détente and it is therefore essential that the proper direction be followed from the outset. This is a fundamental issue, extending far beyond the question of emigration.

I believe that we ought to press our traditional commitment to human rights in the emerging détente not only because this commitment is a most solemn pledge, not only because these values are right in themselves, but because it must be a purpose of the détente to bring the Soviet Union into the community of civilized nations, to hasten the end of what Sakharov has called, "an intolerable isolation, bringing with it the ugliest consequences." The isolation of the Soviet Union, which, in Sakharov's words, "is highly perilous for all mankind, for international confidence and détente," is as dangerous as and comparable to the isolation of Germany in 1937. In that year, the great German writer Thomas Mann wrote:

> Why isolation, world hostility, lawlessness, intellectual interdict, cultural darkness, and every other evil? Why not rather Germany's voluntary return to the European system,

her reconciliation with Europe, with all the inward accompaniments of freedom, justice, well-being, and human decency, and a jubilant welcome from the rest of the world? Why not? Only because a regime which, in word and deed, denies the rights of man, which wants above all else to remain in power, would stultify itself and be abolished if, since it cannot make war, it actually made peace.

Too often, those who insist that the pace and development of détente should reflect progress in the area of human rights are accused of opposition to détente itself. Nothing could be further from the truth. The argument is not between the proponents and detractors of détente, but between those who wish a genuine era of international accommodation based on progress toward individual liberty and those who, in the final analysis, are indifferent to such progress.

We will have moved from the appearance to the reality of détente when East Europeans can freely visit the West, when Soviet students in significant numbers can come to American universities, and when American students in significant numbers can study in Russia. When reading the Western press and listening to Western broadcasts is no longer an act of treason, when families can be reunited across national borders, when emigration is free—then we shall have a genuine détente between peoples and not a formula between governments for capitulation on the issue of human rights.

Without bringing about an increasing measure of individual liberty in the communist world, there can be no genuine détente, there can be no real movement toward a more peaceful world. If we permit form to substitute for substance, if we are content with what in Washington is referred to as "atmospherics," we will not only fail to keep our own most solemn promises, we will, in the long run, fail to keep the peace.

Senator Henry M. Jackson of Washington is a member of the Armed Services Committee.

Relations With Our Adversaries

Marshall D. Shulman

In the six and a half years that have passed since the second *Pacem in Terris* convocation, substantial changes have taken place in America's relations with its two principal adversaries, the Soviet Union and the People's Republic of China. Transformations which were regarded by many in 1967 as visionary or remote have been realized, the effect of which has been to introduce a new period in international politics. So dramatically and so swiftly have these events come upon us that we have not yet a clear understanding as to how deep or how durable are the changes that have taken place, nor a clear idea of the requirements and the possibilities of the new period. We can appreciate that the changes are both radical and yet limited; that they require less simplistic terms of analysis than we have been using; and that they confront us with the need for fresh thought about the objectives of our foreign policies.

In the case of China, twenty-three years of isolation have given way to limited contacts. The representation of the People's Republic of China in the United Nations and the presence of her representatives on the world diplomatic stage are limited but significant steps toward Chinese participation in the international community. Fundamental differences in outlook persist between

China and the United States, but high-level visits symbolize the recognition of the existence of some common
interests between the two countries and some modulation
in the stark and hostile stereotypes by which they had
characterized each other.

In the case of the Soviet Union, twenty-six years of
fluctuating tension and hostility have yielded to an
ambiguous mixture of competition, restraint and limited
cooperation, which the two countries have agreed to call
"peaceful coexistence." It is recognized that this term
does not have the same significance for the two countries,
and that fundamental differences in objectives continue
in force, but what appears to be understood in common
is that tensions are maintained at lower levels, some
common interests are recognized, and at least a partial
codification of the terms of competition is accepted.
Notably reduced is the emotional exacerbation of differences between the two countries which, in the climate of
anxieties of the immediate postwar period, served to
stamp these differences as absolute and intractable.
Although the Strategic Arms Limitation Talks have not
yet substantially constrained the competition in strategic
weapons, they have begun a process which may have
useful educational effects and which expresses a common
interest in the avoidance of general nuclear war. The
expansion of trade, cultural exchanges and functional
cooperation in science, technology and environmental
problems are regarded by the political leadership of both
countries as elements of a growing network of
interdependency.

Are these changes temporary and tactical, or will
they continue in force and lead to more substantial
improvements in these adversary relationships? The
answer rests in large part upon tenuous balances in the
domestic politics of each of the three countries. Those
who follow political developments in Peking generally
report the impression, based upon very limited infor-

mation, that the range of possible trends in the post-Mao situation extend over a full 180 degrees—from a continued development of diplomatic contacts and an effort to emphasize the economic development of the country, to a return to militancy and isolation. Although logic would seem to argue for the former course, the uncertainty resides in the possible range of coalitions that may dominate the internal politics of China, and the bureaucratic pressures involved.

The internal politics of the Soviet Union appear to be deeply preoccupied with the operational problems of a period of reduced tension in foreign policy. The ascendant view is based upon the priority consideration of the needs of the economy for substantial imports from abroad of grain, consumer goods, machinery, technology and capital; against these economic interests are ranged the orthodox wing of the Party bureaucracy, the large and influential police security apparatus, and certain military interests. The resultant compromise has enabled the leadership to pursue a foreign policy of reduced tension, while the security apparatus and the Party bureaucracy have accelerated efforts to contain and cauterize the possible effects of increased contacts with the West upon their system of centralized political control. From the point of view of the outside world, the effect has been to heighten the contradiction between "peaceful coexistence" and the sharpening of the ideological struggle, and between reduced tension on the international plane and a heightening of domestic repression in the cultural and intellectual spheres of Soviet life. It is difficult to judge from the outside what the threshold of viability may be for the present leadership, and the balance of conflicting domestic interests is, therefore, problematical.

Domestic politics in the United States reflects a challenge to present foreign policy from two contradictory philosophical directions. One tendency in American thought emphasizes the importance of achieving security through increasing military strength; it weighs the advantages of a "peaceful coexistence" relationship with the Soviet Union as being largely on the Soviet side, and fears that the increase in economic relations, in cultural contacts, and in arms limitation negotiations will result in a relative increase in the Soviet power position. It is skeptical of the Soviet turn toward "peaceful coexistence" as representing anything more than a temporary tactic, and it tends to think of relations with the Soviet Union as analogous to the experience with the Nazis before World War II. Associated with this view are military interests groups and the conservative and nationalist segment of the spectrum of American politics. From the other side of the spectrum, the present course is challenged by those who react with abhorrence to the regressive domestic trends in Soviet politics. Responsive to the pleas of Soviet intellectuals and the plight of Jews and other Soviet minority groups, they question on moral grounds the development of relations with a Soviet leadership that maintains its system of control by strengthened measures of repression, intensified emphasis upon an ideology of conflict, and a minimum and controlled response to the widening of cultural contacts with the outside world.

The interplay of these domestic pressures in each of the three countries is however constrained by the effect of underlying forces bearing upon them, what the Soviets would call the "objective forces" of the situation. For the Chinese, a policy of widening contacts and flexibility offers some protection against the dangers they perceive from the Soviet Union, and the prospect of help in strengthening the Chinese economic base. For the Soviet Union, a policy of reduced tension is a logical response to the need for an influx of goods and technology from abroad, the alternative to which would be politically divisive reforms in the Soviet economic and political system. Also, the present course offers some prospect of averting an accelerated, more costly and dangerous competition in strategic weapons, and some hope of increasing Soviet political influence in Europe and Japan, in consolidating its control position in Eastern Europe, and in limiting the dangers it perceives from China. In a general sense, the present course represents a culmination of twenty years of effort to shake off the liabilities and dysfunctional effects of the Stalinist legacy in Soviet foreign policy. For the United States, the movement toward improved relations with its adversaries represents a response to the risks and costs of the military competition, a reduced drain upon the economy in a time of economic duress, a strong inclination toward a reduction of commitments abroad, a preoccupation with domestic social and political problems, and pressures from the private interests of segments of the business community.

In the light of these "objective factors," as modified by the play of domestic politics in the three countries, it seems likely that the development of relations with China and the Soviet Union may follow its own dialectical course, inflected from time to time toward greater or lesser tension, but unlikely to return to the extremes of unmitigated hostility which characterized the past two decades.

The starting point for an effort to clarify U.S. objectives in relation to its adversaries is the distinction between our immediate and our long-term purposes. There can be no doubt but that our major purpose in the immediate period is to reduce the hazard of general nuclear war. The general complacency about the possibilities of nuclear war, stemming from our habituation to the nuclear age and the unthinkability of the scale of destruction of nuclear warfare, is not warranted. This complacency rests upon an assumption of rationality in national decision-making for which recent historical experience gives little confidence. The prospect of the widespread availability of fissionable materials and nuclear technology to additional countries and to terrorist groups, the possibility of technical mishap or unauthorized action by military personnel, and the danger of involvement of the nuclear powers in local conflict situations, all should remind us that the present, potentially unstable balance of nuclear deterrence is at best a tenuous basis for preserving the peace. From this, it would follow that the main short-term objective in our relations with our adversaries should be to moderate and stabilize the military competition, and to strengthen restraints against great-power exploitation of local conflict situations. Unless this immediate objective is achieved, all other objectives are without meaning.

At the same time, there should be a present consciousness that our main long-term objective in these relationships is to draw our adversaries into constructive participation in the international system. In this sense, we understand the international system to *mean a codification of civilized practices among nations,* not for the purpose of preserving the status quo—which, in this time of rapid and profound change, would be an impossible task—but for the purpose of assuring that the process of change among nations can be as orderly as possible, with a minimum of violence, and a maximal respect for the wishes of the people involved. If we define our national interest in broad and enlightened terms, the strengthening of the international system in this sense must surely be the paramount purpose of our foreign policy, and it would follow that our principal purpose in relation to our adversaries would be to encourage them, over time, to see their own self-interest and security in this kind of an international environment. We recognize that our adversaries do not now share this view, that their ultimate political objectives are quite different from our own. It is precisely this difference which defines the adversary relationship, rather than any territorial conflict of interest. We do not minimize the profound transformations in the Chinese and Soviet political systems and ideological commitments that will be required if these countries are to be brought to a common acceptance of an international system based upon international law and strengthened international mechanisms, providing for peaceful and orderly processes of change.

What is at issue is not communism versus capitalism, or the right of the people of China and the Soviet Union to organize their societies, their system of the ownership of property, or their political system as they wish. It is not a question of converting our adversaries to capitalism or the two-party system, or of achieving a convergence in our forms of domestic organization. Both they and we are likely to evolve considerably in the coming decades, each in accordance with its own historical traditions and political culture. In that evolution, what we need to strive for is a recognition by all parties of the reality that imperialism and hegemony are anachronisms in today's world, that they cannot provide the basis for a stable and secure world order. Conflicts of interest among nations will, of course, continue so long as nations exist. What makes these conflicts unmanageable is the commitment of nations to an ideology of ultimate hostility and unending struggle, and so long as such ideologies are rooted in the organizational life of political systems and are regarded as vital necessities for the maintenance of power by political leaderships and their apparatus of control, there will be limits on the possibility of the reduction of tension among nations and the peacefulness of their co-existence.

Therefore, it would follow that, while it is possible and desirable to moderate the hostility and codify the terms of competition with our adversaries as they now are in the interest of reducing the hazard of nuclear war, our long-term objective of drawing our adversaries into constructive participation in an international system of this kind will depend upon substantial transformations in the organizational and ideological commitments of our adversaries, as well as a considerable change in our own behavior.

If our purposes are correctly understood as reducing the danger of nuclear war in the present situation while we set in motion longer-term changes in the direction of a fundamental moderation of the adversary relationships, what policies would best serve these objectives? The following guidelines, briefly stated, are offered as a basis for discussion:

1) Although we recognize that the Soviet Union and China may hope for tactical advantages from "peaceful coexistence," we should nevertheless welcome this turn in Soviet policy, as we have done in the case of China, because it can reduce the danger of war, because we can compete effectively on these grounds, and because it opens the way to more substantial transformations in the relationship.

2) We should seek a military equilibrium in both strategic and conventional weapons, as stable and at as moderate a level as can be achieved by negotiations, with the long-term purpose in mind of moving beyond security by deterrence to international security mechanisms, as changes in present commitments to national sovereignty make these feasible.

3) We should make it clear that the function of this military balance is to negate the use or threat of force, and we should seek to strengthen the commitment to non-intervention by force to prevent or encourage political change, as an essential principle of the international system.

4) While every expansion of Soviet or Chinese influence is not necessarily a threat to our interests, we should seek by political and economic means to strengthen our ties with countries that share our values

and our commitment to an international system, and assist independent nations to maintain their autonomy and improve the conditions of life for their people.

5) Recognizing that the desire for an expansion of economic relations is an important motivation for the present Soviet policy, and that this interest can encourage restraint in conflict areas, we should respond affirmatively at modest levels, with a slowly sloping increase over the coming decade as conditions warrant.

6) In the realm of cultural relations, we should seek to maximize the free exchange of people and ideas in accordance with prevailing practices among non-communist nations, and should not resign ourselves to, nor emulate, the centralized controls over cultural exchanges by political and police authorities now characteristic of our adversaries.

7) We should make manifestly clear our belief that there is a fundamental inconsistency between the development of "peaceful coexistence" and the "sharpening of the ideological struggle," and should insist that the competition between conflicting political ideas is best expressed in the performance of the respective systems.

8) Although the present network of bilateral agreements for functional cooperation in the fields of science, technology and the environment is limited to common concerns now regarded as peripheral, we should seek to increase and widen these measures of cooperation, in the expectation that the growing appreciation of the centrality of these concerns will contribute to fundamental transformations in the relationships.

9) Although we recognize the legitimacy of the Soviet security interest in not having hostile regimes on its European border, and should make it clear that we do not intend to use force to bring about changes in this area, we should also make it clear that we regard a Soviet hegemonical sphere in Eastern Europe as an anachronism, and should encourage the Soviet Union to accept the

participation of these states in normal forms of functional association with their European neighbors.

10) While the opening of contacts with the People's Republic of China has served to accelerate Soviet interests in improving relations with the United States, we should make it clear that we would regard the further exacerbation of the Sino-Soviet conflict as a dangerous and undesirable development, and that our ultimate interest is to encourage both countries to move toward moderation and restraint in their foreign policies.

We have seen that the operational problems of trying to contain the effects of a low-tension foreign policy have led the Soviet regime to intensify its controls over the spiritual and intellectual life of its people, and this has provoked an agonizing discussion in this country of whether our interest in peaceful relations with the Soviet Union obliges us to ignore or appear to condone these increased violations of human rights in the Soviet Union. Some have expressed dismay that a "normalization" of relations should have had regressive effects in Soviet domestic life. Others have gone further, and asserted that a régime that behaves in this fashion at home cannot be a reliable or trustworthy partner in international undertakings; and some argue that our government should make it a condition for the development of economic relations that the Soviet Union allow unrestricted emigration and desist from its more egregious police actions against its citizens.

To sort out our thoughts on these matters is difficult at the outset because we do not have a clear answer to the analytical question whether there is a direct or an inverse relationship between a reduction of international tension and progress toward liberalization within the Soviet system. It is possible that despite the regressive tightening of controls, the long-term effect of reduced tension and increased contacts will be the irresistible growth of pressures for curbing the police apparatus. It is also possible that the significant pressures for change may come, not merely from the handful of articulate and courageous dissidents, but from within the system itself, as it seeks to rid itself of these encumbrances to productivity, initiative and modernization. We can only speculate; we cannot know whether progress toward advanced industrialization will make for a more efficient technocratic dictatorship, or whether it will encourage the growth of pluralism and a separation of the society from the all-embracing control of the state. Perhaps one can venture the judgment that a prolonged period of reduced international tension and increased contacts may encourage trends toward genuine constitutionalism and respect for human rights; whereas a period of heightened international tension will almost certainly not do so.

In our response to these matters, it is necessary to distinguish between the role of our government and the role of individuals and private groups. The United States government is properly concerned with the foreign policy of the Soviet Union, and with those aspects of its domestic life which bear directly and demonstrably upon its foreign policy—such as its treatment of American citizens in the Soviet Union, its encouragement of hostile propaganda or the level of Soviet military preparations. As individuals and as members of private groups, we can and we should express our humanitarian concern over the repugnant aspects of the Soviet system, for the barbaric throttling of the creative life of its intellectuals and artists by a large and unconstrained police apparatus. But if this expression of concern is to carry conviction, it must be applied even-handedly. Our protests against the disregard of the United Nations Declaration of Human Rights in the Soviet Union must be without self-righteousness and based upon principle—which is to say that our concerns must also be directed against violations of human rights of whatever degree and wherever they occur—whether in countries allied to us, or here at home. Otherwise, the motivation for these protests is suspect, and our moral commitment is clouded.

In practice, the government cannot of course wholly detach itself from the sentiments of the people. Though it must direct its efforts in the first instance to the priority concern for reducing the danger of nuclear war, and though it must avoid public and frontal demands upon the Soviet Union in regard to domestic affairs, it can make it perfectly clear in its private communications that it cannot ignore the manifest concern of a large segment of the American public lest our actions appear to condone the flaunted cynicism of the Soviet police apparatus. One can hope that the Soviet leadership will recognize that it would be a miscalculation to believe that the "normalization" of its external relations can be totally separated from the excesses of its police bureaucracy at home.

The lesson of this experience may be a useful one for the American people. In the past, we have been prone to think of the Soviet Union in terms of simplistic extremes. During World War II, the Soviet Union was our "gallant ally" and it was thought harmful to the war effort to see any blemishes or to think about the problems that lay ahead. During the Cold War, the picture was unmitigatedly black. Perhaps we are now better prepared to live with a more differentiated picture in our minds. We have achieved the first step in moderating tensions and encouraging restraint in our competition. It is a limited step, but an important one—potentially a historic turning point. We must now find within ourselves the maturity to live for a long time with an ambiguous mixture of deadly serious competition between two countries of greatly differing values and purposes, which nevertheless have some interests in common, the most important of which is to bring some sanity into their military competition.

Marshall D. Shulman is Professor of Government and Director, Russian Institute, Columbia University

II

THE JACKSON AMENDMENT:
PRO AND CON

Senator Henry M. Jackson's demand that the U.S. force concessions from the Soviet Union on internal policy as an adjunct of détente provoked spirited debate at Pacem in Terris III. *Here are excerpts from comments offered by panelists at several of the following sessions.*

Fred Warner Neal:

This is a conference not only about foreign policy but about politics. Politics means compromises, not necessarily on long-range goals but certainly on tactics and shorter-term results. Politics also involves decisions about priorities. Practically, that is what both politics and morality are about, every day.

In terms of American foreign policy, we must see that it is the Cold War which has been a block to realistic American positions. There is no need to argue here about who is most to blame for the Cold War, or why. It is enough to say that the Nixon-Kissinger shift away from Cold War policy and attitudes is the most constructive foreign policy development since the end of World War II. And those who desire to serve the best interests of the United States—not only our best interests in terms of national security but our best interests also in terms of moral principle—should support this Nixon-Kissinger policy, regardless of Watergate, partisan politics, Jewish emigration, Soviet dissidents or anything else.

What this means in terms of immediate practical politics is opposition to the Jackson amendment to the pending trade bill. Senator Jackson is at least consistent.

He always has been a Cold Warrior. Some of those now with him have not been so identified. I think they are being misled. What Senator Jackson is doing—intentionally or unintentionally—amounts to an attempt to continue the Cold War by other means.

I find myself confused by the sudden and somewhat mysterious popularity of the Universal Declaration of Human Rights. I am pleased about it in one way, but I think it means something more than meets the eye. If we are really concerned about it and think we can produce democracy, American style, all over the world through our foreign policy, surely there is—literally—a world of opportunity for us to demonstrate our high moral principle in places where we might be able to have some effect. I doubt that the Soviet Union is one of these places. I disapprove of many Soviet policies, and I hope the U.S.S.R. will change them. But so far as they concern Soviet internal affairs, it is not our business to try to force changes. Practically, we can't do it. The idea of the United States being able to reform the Soviet Union to conform to our own image simply by continuing to discriminate against it in foreign trade is preposterous.

What we can do is contribute to world conditions which will make it possible—and more likely—for the U.S.S.R. to develop domestic policies to which we can be more amenable. We can do this by continuing the policy of détente, by making it firm, by making sure that the Cold War is firmly and definitively over and in no danger of being revived. Right now, this means not only opposition to the Jackson amendment but to the Jackson amendment psychology.

We have a great chance now—for the first time—to build a rational, realistic foreign policy which can serve not only our security but which can—in the right hands—also further our ideals. That is what *Pacem in Terris* in 1973 is all about.

Fred Warner Neal is Chairman, Faculty in International Relations, Claremont Graduate School, and an Associate of the Center for the Study of Democratic Institutions.

Jerome Alan Cohen:

I do not endorse the Jackson amendment whole-heartedly; instead, I approach it in a way somewhat different from that of Messrs. Kissinger, Shulman and Neal. Let me point out, first of all, that President Nixon has sought to counter the Jackson amendment by saying that its endorsement would be ineffective, illegitimate and unwise. It seems to me that the President is plainly wrong when he suggests that such economic pressure, written into law, is likely to be wholly ineffective with respect to the Soviets. We have already seen some surprising concessions from Moscow in an attempt to placate the Congress so as to enjoy not only the most-favored-nation provisions that the Jackson amendment would deny, but also the very important U.S. credit and investment guarantees which are at stake.

I don't understand Professor Shulman when he argues that the Jackson amendment would be ineffective with the Soviets. Rather, he seems to share the view that its application would be illegitimate and unwise. Unlike Professor Shulman, my own view is that a nation's emigration policy is not exclusively a matter within its domestic jurisdiction, but obviously can have the most profound effect on other countries. It is part of a country's foreign policy, and I don't think it is illegitimate in any way for another government to seek to influence another nation's emigration policy. So I don't think legitimacy is the question. I think it comes down to wisdom.

I must say I share some of Professor Shulman's concerns about the wisdom of the Jackson amendment. I think we have to understand that without this kind of government pressure it is quite unrealistic to expect the Soviet Union to cease its restrictions on the emigration of Jews and other minorities. Just the other day we were told by the Soviet political correspondent, Victor Louis, in *The New York Times* that if people want to leave the Soviet Union to go to other countries, there's usually no problem, but if they want to leave to go to Israel there's a very long line and they have a very long wait. So this seems to be a matter of the discriminatory nature of the Soviet application of its emigration laws.

My problem is that it appears to Professors Shulman and Kissinger, Neal and others that détente is at stake here. Indeed, our nuclear survival, they claim, is at stake if the Jackson amendment is enacted. Détente may be reversed. We may be threatening the world with a holocaust. It seems to me this is intellectual overkill. The Soviet Union has already made clear, as recently as yesterday's *Times*, that it is prepared to adjust to the political realities of this country. It knows the House Ways and Means Committee has already enacted a version of the Jackson amendment. And it is still prepared to carry on trade with us.

My own prediction would be that if the Jackson amendment is enacted the Soviets are likely to yield on the emigration question, at least with respect to its discriminatory application. Even if they don't, they're certainly not going to let this stand in the way of overriding interests in economic cooperation and survival. So I think we have to keep this within realistic ambit, and we shouldn't get too apocalyptic in our statements of what the consequences of the enactment of this amendment are likely to be.

However, I've got my own doubts, which are different from and in addition to those that have been expressed about the Jackson amendment. First of all, as Professor Shulman recognizes, it is desirable for us to be even-handed in our application of standards to the world and to ourselves. Yet the Jackson amendment only applies to non-market economy countries—communist countries. Is it of any lesser concern to the American people that there might be discriminatory emigration controls by South Korea or Taiwan or Greece or Spain—that is, by military capitalistic dictatorships of various kinds? Our concerns should lie not only with the communist world.

It does seem to me that the Jackson amendment should be recast in order to take account of all countries that restrict emigration for racial or religious or ethnic reasons. That would give us a more evenhanded standard. Another point: the amendment as now cast certainly encompasses China, even though the American public has no motivation at this point to withhold from China full access to its markets and possible credits and credit investment guarantees. Perhaps the Chinese are lucky that the Jewish community which was autochthonous to China disappeared by the twentieth century. If today there were hundreds or thousands of Jews clamoring with others to get out of China, we might have a somewhat less rosy view of China than we do.

China, at this stage, unlike the Soviet Union, is still governed by first generation revolutionary leaders. Our détente with China, if one can so describe it, is in a very, very preliminary stage. And I can assure you that, unlike the Soviet situation, it seems very unlikely that any economic pressures at this stage in our relations with China could possibly be effective. So, my feeling is that we've got to be more discriminating, and I find it very unfortunate that the Jackson amendment would certainly include China, even though China's domestic policies are not presently a focus of concern for American public opinion.

Finally, there is another complexity. If all these countries lived up to the provisions of the amendment and would permit complete and unrestrained emigration, what would be the consequences? Can we understand what would happen if millions of people were to pour out of China? How many of our legislators would vote to admit them to the United States? Or to what extent could we legitimately persuade other nations to take them in? In 1962, for a brief period, the People's

Republic did open up its borders and tens of thousands of people poured into Hong Kong, and the British had to quickly close the border after sixty thousand entered. They couldn't assimilate them.

Certainly we should not keep the promise to the ear and break it to the hope, as Shakespeare said. It seems most unfair to come out for unlimited emigration throughout the world and not be able to provide homes for the would-be immigrants. So I would opt for a standard that recasts the Jackson amendment, that recognizes that we should voice universal concerns about emigration, but that we can only implement them to a limited extent. And I would make the denial of trade benefits depend on a presidential finding that a given country in given factual circumstances denies emigration for religious, racial or ethnic reasons only.

Now that's not a perfect formula; one can think of other alternatives. But it seems to me that it is a better solution to our current dilemma than no action—which my hardheaded friends in the world of international politics seem to think appropriate—or the Jackson amendment, which I think is using a blunderbuss to kill a flea.

Jerome Alan Cohen is Director, East Asian Legal Studies, Harvard Law School.

John Paton Davies:

Professor Shulman devotes little more than two paragraphs and scattered references to China in his address. His attention is directed to the Soviet Union. This strikes me as about the right ratio of emphasis in a discussion of adversaries in this phase of history.

China today is essentially inward-looking. And when its gaze turns outward, it focuses primarily on what Peking perceives to be a Soviet military menace. For us,

China poses no imminent threat. Rather, it is a welcome counterweight to the Soviet Union in a triangular balance of power relationship. What China's government and policies will be after Mao, after Chou, and after the further cultural revolutions we are promised—if they occur—can only be guessed at. So, for the time being, we may concentrate on our ominous relations with the U.S.S.R.

For all of the reasons put forward by Professor Shulman, we want détente, peaceful coexistence with the Soviet Union. They are grave reasons of vital importance not only to us but to all humanity. The Soviet Union, too, wants peaceful coexistence, we assume, for reasons of survival. It also wants a détente for economic reasons. Hobbled and tethered by doctrine, the Soviet economy is backward. The U.S.S.R. needs American economic aid so greatly that the Kremlin is willing to run what it believes to be a risk inherent in peaceful coexistence. That risk is infection of the Soviet system by democratic ideas brought in through contact with the West. The Kremlin has so little confidence in the natural immunities of the Soviet system that it fears such contamination would cripple the "leading role of the Party" and thereby mortally damage the whole system.

So the Kremlin must administer a prophylaxis to this risk. This takes the form of intensified "ideological struggle," in fiercer ideological repression inside the Soviet Union. Ideological struggle is described as a contradiction to peaceful coexistence, but for the Kremlin, in practical terms, it is an essential *complement* to peaceful coexistence. It is the internal repression necessary to compensate for outward relaxation. And it means cruel and unusual punishment and terrorization of those of independent mind, those pleading for elementary human rights.

We have, in effect, made a deal with the Kremlin. It grants us a détente. We, in turn, with expectations of profit to American business, sell grain to feed the Kremlin's subjects (thus far at a cost to the American taxpayer), provide capital and technology, and so build up Soviet strength. We do all of this knowing that it means paranoiac persecution of the most humanistic people in the Soviet Union.

Instances of governments oppressing and persecuting their people, of course, abound. But the case of Soviet repressions of its finest people is so directly connected to our relations with Russia's rulers that our conscience is inescapably involved.

We comfort our conscience with two thoughts. One is the long-term benefits that may ensue from a prolonged détente, if only expressions of our conscience do not intrude to vex the Kremlin. Then there are the more pressing issues, such as arms limitations that might be jeopardized by our acting strongly on conscience.

Stated generally, our long-term objective is, as Professor Shulman pointed out, "to draw our adversaries into constructive participation in the international system." This, he warned, "will depend upon substantial transformations" on the other side. We should recognize that this is no compliment to the Soviet oligarchy, to suggest that it holds doctrine so lightly that it would accede to a mellowing process. It is against the nature of the Soviet régime to ameliorate the adversary relationship. Mutual hostility is an article of doctrine and faith. The Kremlin is alert to our desire gradually to erode its commitment to struggle. In its estimate, we scheme to subvert and corrupt, to weaken its ideological vigor. And so the Kremlin hugs doctrine. Not only out of conviction; also because ideology provides the only semblance of legitimacy and respectability to institutionalized tyranny.

The other comfort to our conscience is that a hope of saving mankind from nuclear destruction is a greater cause than saving Sakharov and Solzhenitsyn from the

KGB. Stating our moral dilemma in those terms, obviously the Soviet dissidents are of lesser concern.

The dilemma, however, is not so stark. And what, in my opinion, we should now ask is so modest that it cannot compromise the exigent Soviet need for peaceful coexistence. We do not ask that the Kremlin allow the American Civil Liberties Union to have free rein in Russia, nor demand that Soviet intellectuals be permitted to publish without censorship. What we now do ask at least—and how little it seems—is that the oligarchy stop affronting the civilized world with savage abuse of its most worthy subjects.

I would like to add that I am troubled by a good deal I hear which assumes the Soviet Union has so drastically changed that ideology can be dismissed as something that is withering away. I think this pays no compliment whatsoever to the Soviet ruling groups, for which ideology is a matter of faith and doctrine; and this is based on a fundamental hostility to us.

John Paton Davies is a former member of the China Policy Planning Staff, U.S. Department of State.

Neal:

One word on Mr. Davies' last point. I don't think anybody suggested—at least I didn't say, or mean to imply—that the Soviet Union has abandoned its ideology. I think some aspects of its ideology have been altered and some concepts have changed. This is important. But if you are saying that the Soviets are still dedicated to a communist world and thus oppose capitalism, of course you are correct. They are unlikely to love us, or even to snuggle up to us. But there is nothing in the fundamental Soviet ideology which impels them to commit military aggression against us. Our new policy of détente has apparently recognized this, at long last.

Davies:

My point is that Soviet ideology poses a basic hostility to the United States and a belief that it will last. And I am surprised that I don't see more recognition that there is a continuing underlying animosity, and that détente is a tactic. There would be a danger of illusion if we don't keep it in mind.

Hans J. Morgenthau:

The balance of power doesn't operate in a vacuum but within a model universe which approves morally the principle of the balance of power itself. This moral context which existed not so much in the nineteenth century, as always mentioned, but in the eighteenth century, has disappeared. I would say, however, that the Jackson amendment is an attempt to recreate a modicum of modern consensus with regard to certain fundamental principles of behavior, which is a precondition for a viable and volatile peer system. So I find nothing of a moralistic crusade, or of uncalled-for intervention into domestic affairs of other nations in those attempts to mitigate the totalitarian character, and more particularly the xenophobic character of the Soviet régime.

I fully agree with the wisdom of academician Sakharov's statement in support of the Jackson amendment that détente in a fundamental sense depends upon a moral context to which the participants of the détente adhere. In my own contacts with Russian intellectuals and diplomats, which have been quite frequent but have now virtually ceased, I have found this moral gap between somebody who is capable, at least within certain limits, of speaking his mind without adverse consequences, and somebody who has been trained like a Pavlovian dog to respond mechanically to orders of the government.

I find the Russian elite's ignorance of the American political processes an enormous impediment to a real understanding. If you read, for instance, the recent book by Anatoli Gromyko, the son of the Foreign Minister of the Soviet Union, who is head of the Foreign Policy section of the American Institute of the Soviet Academy of Sciences and the Minister-Counsellor-designate in Washington, you are simply flabbergasted by the utter nonsense which a learned, well-informed, and, I suppose, intelligent man presents as the objective truth. To give you one example: he writes about the Kennedy years, and he explains certain changes in Kennedy's foreign policy by the competition between the Eastern and Western American monopolies. Now I've never heard of competition within monopolies which seems to me to be a contradiction in terms; but let this pass. This is important perhaps for a freshman class but not in high politics. The idea of reducing Kennedy to an agent of Eastern capitalists, and explaining any deviation from whatever he calls a Kennedy line as a deviation among the capitalists themselves—the bankers and the industrialists—seems to me to be plainly absurd.

Where you have such a situation, the opening up of a totalitarian system so that its people can at least glimpse something of the outside world or have a limited chance to test the official interpretation of events with another interpretation of events, is a precondition for a working system of the balance of power.

Hans J. Morgenthau is Leonard Davis Distinguished Professor of Political Science, City University of New York.

III

WHAT IS THE
NATIONAL INTEREST?

The foregoing exchange did not end the debate over the issues raised by the Jackson amendment, but it was useful in leading to the presentation by three scholars of their views on the U.S. national interest in a broader context. Stanley Hoffmann, emphasizing changes in the international system, rules out both a continuation of the Cold War policy and a return to isolationism, and addresses himself to "flaws and omissions" in the Nixon-Kissinger policy. Richard J. Barnet, continuing the analysis, sees policy changes primarily in Washington rather than in Peking and Moscow and warns that the real threat to American security is domestic rather than foreign. Robert W. Tucker discerns no serious effort to change either the concept of American interests or American commitments. Arguing that peace is now divisible, rather than indivisible, he emphasizes that dependence is not necessarily a desirable condition and that interdependence is not necessarily productive of peace.

Flaws and Omissions in the
New Foreign Policy

Stanley Hoffmann

The problem of the national interest is even more complex today than in the years when the provocative writings of Hans Morgenthau led to a thorough discussion of this concept. In the new circumstances of the 1970s, three questions must be asked.

1) The first concerns the frame of reference. Is the American national interest shaped primarily by the international system, by the varieties of threats and opportunities, commitments and concerns, material and psychological investments and expectations *outside* the borders of the U.S.? This was, to a very large extent, how the national interest was defined after World War II (despite the pronouncements of most of the "revisionist" historians of the Cold War, eager to find its roots in the needs of the domestic system). Not exclusively, to be sure: for instance, the American refusal, during the period 1945-47, to accept a simple division of the world into spheres of influence—as suggested by Stalin—had a great deal to do with traditional American ideals and images about the world and about America's mission. But even if external pressures and problems were turned into imperatives and policies by domestically-based conceptions (or misconceptions), it was the events on the world

scene, however misinterpreted, that shaped the definition of U.S. foreign policy.

One may ask whether this is still the case. To what extent is foreign policy now shaped by domestic priorities, demands and fears? Or at least by the need not to move beyond what domestic opinion tolerates, and not to ignore what internal interests require? If this is the case today, one would have to conclude, not, as several more or less Marxist writers have stated, that the nature of American capitalism determines American foreign policy, but that the present condition of the U.S. economic system (its increasing dependence on outside raw materials and energy, its comparative loss of dynamism in a world of fierce competition for exports of consumer goods, of advanced technology, of foodstuffs, and also of arms) is likely to dictate policies which would have been inconceivable some years ago. This is a very important question. For we have emerged from the Cold War with what might be called an "American system" in the world—a network of explicit alliances, open or discreet protectorates, economic and political investments, and international charters and agencies reflecting American preferences and interests, e.g., G.A.T.T., Bretton Woods, etc. If the national interest were defined exclusively by external necessities, much of this system could be found, at present, superfluous, obsolete or even counter-productive. But if a growing segment of the U.S. economy, and also much of the machinery of government (not just the security agencies but the quasi-monarchic Executive itself) depend for their health or survival on the preservation or restoration of this world system, then we are likely to get a very different perspective on the national interest—and to find resistance to drastic change much greater.

2) Even more than in the 1950s, the word "national" raises a host of questions. Not only, to be sure, for the U.S. Soviet foreign policy has often had to choose

between the interests of the U.S.S.R. as a country, and that of the Soviet Union as a cause, to borrow the late U.S. Ambassador to the U.S.S.R. Charles E. Bohlen's distinction. (Usually, the former has prevailed, but the Soviets have acted with particular determination when the two coincided, as in Czechoslovakia). In America's case, for reasons provided by a combination of institutional pluralism and ideological idealism, two sets of dilemmas are created by the term "national." On the one hand, there is the distinction between the interest of the U.S. as an entity, a "cold monster" concerned only with its needs and entitlements as a state, and the interests of private U.S. establishments all over the world. In an international system in which, for instance, multinational corporations have budgets larger than many states and can undermine the monetary autonomy of all states, the statesman's predicament becomes acute. For he cannot act as the ideal-typical diplomat of the nineteenth century was supposed to have acted, i.e., without reference to domestic private interests. These are simply too large, too essential to the prosperity and even prestige of the nation to be left out of state calculations. And yet, to identify their concerns with the national interest, and to capitulate to their pressures, for instance on matters of expropriation abroad, or over Middle East policy, would be a perfect recipe for trouble. The very importance of the chessboards on which private groups are players of international relations obliges statesmen to expand their notion of the national interest; but at the same time it risks being dissolved and prostituted.

On the other hand, there is the choice between defining the national interest as if the "game" were going to remain a contest of nation-states (or empires)—each one having, therefore, the duty to play its cards as skillfully, and to defend its stakes as forcefully as possible—and defining it as if the new world of the last third of this century needed to bring mankind "beyond the nation-state" for all the reasons of economic interdependence and nuclear terror, of nation-state incapacity and transnational groups' irresponsibility, with which we are familiar. At times, one may be tempted to say that almost by definition statesmen necessarily choose the former approach, for a narrow definition is their *raison d'être,* a broad one would put them out of business. And yet, the flaws of the narrow approach are unmistakable.

3) A third question results from the change in the international system. It is relatively easy to define the national interest in two sets of cases. The first one is that of a clear and compelling external threat, which dictates priorities, disciplines internal interests, dampens dissent and mobilizes energies. The second one is that of states in a balance-of-power system. Each major actor has an interest in preventing any rival from going too far, and in not going so far as to provoke a coalition of its rivals; each small actor has an interest in using the great powers' rivalry to protect its integrity. For more than twenty-five years, the U.S. has lived in the first of these two systems. Its leaders now take credit for having brought it to an end. But the result is not the emergence of "a classical balance of power," as the 1973 State of the World message acknowledges; the world of the 1970s does not fulfill the conditions of a balance-of-power system. We are condemned to innovate. This is a world where military might is not the daily, manifest criterion of power and influence; in which other forms of power play an increasing role; in which "security" means not only safety from armed attack or subversion, but also safety from internal collapse due to political *or* to economic and environmental disasters, and safe access to necessary resources either abroad or within one's borders, i.e., no foreign domination. World politics now takes the form of contests played on different chessboards, with different coalitions and rules on each, yet also with complex and

often unpredictable "linkages." In other words, it is a world for which the so-called wisdom of the ages, and the constructs of scholars, provide really no compass.

In so dubious a battle, only two things are clearly ruled out. The first one is a perpetuation of the Cold War policy. Not only have we lost the essential prerequisite— the existence, and the myth, of a monolithic enemy (the myth lasted longer than the reality, yet is alive no more); but the strains which the compulsion of manning the barricades all over the world imposed on America's material and psychological resources had become unbearable—in part only because of Vietnam. The second way of defining the national interest that must be ruled out, despite the songs of some brilliant sirens, is isolationism. It is true that the stability of deterrence insures the physical security of the U.S.; that this security would not be threatened even if a repudiation of U.S. military commitments abroad led to an epidemic of neutralism among ex-allies or to a sharp increase of Soviet or Chinese influence; that the needs of the U.S. economy could continue to be met if the U.S. ended its military or political support of "moderate" or friendly régimes abroad. But there are three reasons why such arguments are not likely to be convincing. There is the fear—justified or not—of the price tag of a hostile world for U.S. imports and exports (even if oil-producing countries would still have to sell oil to us, they could charge ever more prohibitive rates). And would U.S. investments in the Common Market be safe in a "Finlandized" Western Europe? There is the fact that no great power has ever defined its interest in terms of physical security alone; influence is the name of the game—even more so when the blunt play of might becomes too risky, and especially so when the great power stands for, or thinks it stands for, certain ideals or principles of behavior. And there is the existence of what I have called "the U.S. world system." It is simply too vast, too intricate; it crystallizes too many interests within the U.S. and abroad to be dismantled and abandoned in the sweeping way the neo-isolationist thesis suggests. Even if such a demolition job were desirable, I doubt it could be done deliberately.

In between these two extremes, the Administration has offered its own version of the national interest. It is not exactly easy to define. Since the reconquest of freedom of maneuver for Gulliver was clearly one of the chief aims of Nixon and Kissinger, one cannot be too critical of the way in which their exercise of this freedom has made it very difficult to find out exactly what they think America's interests and the ideal world system are. Their resort to secrecy, surprise and ambiguity reminds one of another statesman for whom freedom of maneuver and the avoidance of fixed positions were essential: De Gaulle. Let us, therefore, simply say that four and a half years of Nixon-Kissinger policy suggest the following: It is the *minimum* reconversion of America's external commitments compatible with internal demands for change. Therefore, this reconversion is more spectacular in Southeast Asia than in, say, Western Europe; and far more so in trade and monetary matters than in military ones. It is also the *maximum* reconversion compatible with the desire to preserve as much of America's world primacy as possible. Thus, neither the accommodation with the chief communist powers, nor the economic warfare against Japan and Western Europe have been pushed so far as to endanger NATO or the Security Treaty with Japan, and the Nixon Doctrine represents not a repudiation of commitments, but a redistribution of burdens.

The great skill of this policy lies in its capacity to offer something for everyone. It points to tangible achievements in arms control. It also pushes arms sales abroad, and new weapons systems within. It proclaims its determination to free the U.S. from "unfair" burdens, whether in alliance costs, or in the status of the dollar, or in world trade. It also continues to pay tribute to alliance solidarity, to the ideal of liberalized trade, to that of a new and stable world monetary system or of a world régime for the high seas. It negotiates explicit or tacit codes of good behavior with its main adversaries. It also resorts freely to unilateral moves or "benign neglect" at its friends' expense. It pulls out troops from Vietnam, Taiwan and Korea. But it props up Israel, Iran or Greece with sophisticated weaponry. It defines the national interest more aggressively or selfishly than earlier. Yet it still identifies it with building "a global structure of peace." There isn't a part of the world, or an issue, about which it could not say, simultaneously, "See how far we have come from the shackles, perils or pitfalls of the Cold War days," and "See how carefully we have, in totally new circumstances, preserved what we had inherited from past Administrations." I am convinced that this period will be seen as a grand transition. But it is not clear to what. Its success depends on the vindication of so many guesses and gambles about the behavior of adversaries and the capacities of allies (for instance, in Indochina), about the ability of the U.S. to manipulate so many variables and pull so many strings in the right direction, that the observer can do little more than hold his breath. But if one is concerned with the long run, maybe one way of indicating where an alternative might be found is to point out two kinds of flaws in the current policy.

1) First, it is riddled with internal tensions and contradictions. They have been manageable so far, but one, which explains all the others, is the inherent instability of a policy of indirect primacy: a neo-Bismarckian attempt at getting others to "do more," but at keeping for us the role of defining what they ought to do or not to do, and of providing them with the tools they need. What happens if they insist on playing their own game and choosing their own tracks? What happens if we miscalculate the moves and maneuvers designed at

keeping them on ours? (Let us remember Bangladesh, or think ahead about South Vietnam and Cambodia; the examples could be multiplied). There is, therefore, a permanent question mark about the "U.S. world system." Can it be controlled and maintained by us, at reduced cost and strain, through others? If those on whom we rely to preserve it: allies, clients, neutrals, and even foes pledged to moderate behavior, should get different ideas, what happens? Do we revert to direct primacy? Do we witness, passively or too late, the transformation of this system into something we do not want, having thus missed the chance of transforming it in time with the cooperation of others? The great art of this Administration has been in making many believe that we had transformed, or were transforming, the "U.S. world system" into a pluralistic, multipolar, "stable structure of peace." In reality, we have only changed the method of operation and control of that system.

Among the contradictions that follow from this, one may list the following: There is one between the search for a détente with Moscow and Peking, and the drive to reassert "Atlantic" solidarity (with Japan somehow added to the family)—as if the sense of common interests among allies was likely to grow as we ourselves assert more keenly than ever the special responsibilities and converging interests of the superpowers. There is the contradiction between treating those allies as partners in security matters and rivals in economic affairs. There is the tension between the self-assertive or unilateralist style and substance of the new policy, and the concern for lasting alliances embracing not only military but political and economic subjects, or the desire for "a stable structure of peace"—as if the resort to shock tactics or the absence of consultation did not both diminish the trust of those whose cooperation we seek, and (as in Western Europe) maximize divisions among those whose unity we say we welcome.

While we call on the West Europeans to unite so as to share the burden more adequately with us in all issues, we tell them that their unity is "not an end in itself" and must be subordinated both to the Atlantic design and our various economic or monetary shocks. The way in which we formulate our demand for a new partnership insures, in fact, that there will be no uniform West European response and that we will continue to deal, separately, with haggling separate states. There is little contradiction between our attempt to get our allies to make economic concessions to us or to increase their financial contributions to the alliances, by exploiting their military dependence on us, and our policy of accommodation with Moscow and Peking; for the more the latter succeeds, the more difficult it will be for us to exploit the "security link"—either because, rightly or wrongly, our allies will feel less threatened by the common foe, or because they will feel threatened by the very collusion of the superpowers and try to react and adjust to it in their own way.

There is another contradiction created by the drive for détente. The Nixon-Kissinger policy depends on executive primacy in the U.S., and has tried to preserve it, just as it has tried to preserve U.S. primacy abroad— but, in the domestic realm, without any reconversion: far from it. An unchecked President, a small, flexible and discreet NSC staff, a Special Assistant with powers of top-level negotiation, an apparatus of secrecy and occasional deception: these are the requirements of the new strategy. Not only do they conflict with the long-term requirements of a "stable international structure." Their domestic legitimacy is being steadfastly undermined by the very success of détente. What may have been necessary in the days of eyeball-to-eyeball confrontation appears far less tolerable when relaxation is both the goal and the achievement. In this respect, just as Vietnam may have cured the U.S. of the excesses of global interventionism, Watergate may purge the political system of the abuses of executive centralization. In both instances, the Nixon-Kissinger policies of détente helped expose the absurdities which made the prolongation of a war—

started for the containment of international communism —so hard to justify, and the perils of the presidential omnipotence which had developed in foreign affairs.

2) After the contradictions, the omissions. There are three very serious ones. The first one concerns what might be called the problem of war control in a moderate international system—how to prevent the resort to nuclear weapons, to eliminate large-scale inter-state violence, and to dampen genocidal domestic violence (with its potential for international involvement) in a world replete with arms, in which the use and accumulation of force still have, alas, a multiplicity of functions (as a means to an end or as an end in itself). The complexity of the problem is such that no grandiose, elegant plans would make any sense; it may require arms control schemes here, balanced rearmament there, collective as well as competitive guarantees, international forces and national means of verification, mixes of neutralization and regional collective security, superpower agreements and an International Security Agency. One thing is sure: the problem requires far more attention than it has received. To be sure, SALT and the coming force reduction talks in Europe are a good beginning. But the détente, insofar as it creates doubts about the U.S. nuclear guarantee to others, may create incentives for proliferation; and nothing has been done to curtail conventional arms races in most of the world. Here, the omission comes partly from the habit of seeing the world security problem essentially in bipolar terms (and while it is true that only two states have the capacity to annihilate the planet, even their own arms race has ceased to be shaped exclusively by each other's fears and calculations). Partly, it results from the habit of considering that the problem of force is inseparable from, and a mere annex to, concrete disputes and discontents, except for the superpowers' strategic arms race which has acquired a life of its own. While it is true that the

problem of force cannot be isolated, this does not justify neglect.

A second omission concerns the third world. There has been a remarkable amount of "decoupling" from its problems and needs, except in two respects. One is the continuing practice of bolstering moderate—often shaky, corrupt or reactionary—régimes on behalf of "stability," largely through military aid and political support. The other is the encouragement of private U.S. investments, despite the resentments they often create and the political embarrassments that may result. Early reactions to the energy crisis seem to oscillate from assumptions of implacable hostility to advocacy of abject support. Obviously, what would be needed here is not a purely American effort, but one in which the industrial powers would all join; not an attempt at dealing with the third world as a bloc, but a willingness to face the diverse issues which are of concern to each nation (and over which they have their own lines of division); not a policy of promoting a grouping of advanced nations confronting all the others, but a policy of cooperation aimed at insuring the full participation in world affairs of states whose absence or discontent would doom any ambition of building a stable world community. Here, the omission stems partly from the American policy-makers' conviction that only the major military or industrial powers matter to world order—that indeed détente reduces the interest of the great powers in the fate of the third world, and the latter's capacity to harm them. It also springs from the nature and pressures of domestic American interests. Whatever the cause, the effect is a serious error. For in the coming international system, there will be other threats to stability than military ones, and huge economic gaps between states in a world full of arms may recreate military perils as well. If the contest of nations remains what it has been in the past, such discrepancies could feed the rivalry of the great powers and drag them into collision. If the peril of force leads to greater prudence, and international politics comes to resemble domestic politics more and more, let us remember that what prevents domestic societies from being destroyed by inequality is mobility at the bottom and redistribution by the top, and that the international milieu, divided into states, has no central mechanism for the latter, and heaps up barriers to the former.

A third omission is implicit in the other two. This is not an Administration that cares much about international agencies. Its very emphasis on asserting purely American interests does not prepare it adequately to pool or delegate sovereignty. And yet, any of the long-term problems that will face mankind—security, the exploitation of resources and oceans, telecommunications and space, the world monetary system, pollution—will require joint action—not merely joint rules of conduct but joint management or joint policy-making, precisely because traditional behavior, i.e., the insistence by states on having the final say, is likely to lead either to chaos, given their lack of adequate control over transnational forces, or to acute conflict, given the highly uneven power relations hidden behind that misleading word, interdependence. Revolts against dependence (on other states or on private groups) may or may not lead to violence, but there are other kinds of disruptions and disasters in the realm of economic affairs. Of course, international agencies do not eliminate dependence, inequality or the power struggle. But they provide mufflers, and may offer solutions. They are no substitute for politics, but—as in domestic societies—they may help replace the politics of brute confrontation with the ritual of bargaining and compromise. Despite some enlightened work in the realm of ocean policy, the Administration has shown very little imagination. The conceptual framework remains traditional: moderating conflicts of states is the highest goal. There is little recognition of the fact that a moderate system, in the future will have to be more than a peaceful *society* of limited partners—it will have to include elements of *community*. Moderation will have to be defined positively as well as negatively, substantially as well as procedurally. For instance, there can be no real moderation with extreme inequality. Thus, in this respect, it is not just the stress on great powers, it is the vision of world politics as simply a competition between states which provides the blinders.

It is not possible here to offer a full-blown alternative—it would be presumptuous and absurd. But the preceding critique suggests certain directions and problems. The contradictions and omissions discussed indicate that we will have to choose between prolonging the present transition, with its acrobatics and its brinkmanship, its hedges and its bets, and transforming the U.S. world system quite drastically. The first alternative is not likely to be "operative," to use the new lingo, not only because of internal strains and damaging deficiencies, but also because of its intimate connection with men who will not be in office forever, and with a system of government whose legitimacy is under sharp attack. The second alternative will have to be a mix. Insofar as world politics remains a contest of states, it will be in our interest to promote a gradual devolution of U.S. privileges, burdens and primacy, so as to encourage a more active participation and a more even distribution of power—in its various forms—both on the global scale and regionally. The requirements, limits and possibilities of such devolution vary considerably from area to area (they are quite different, say, in Western Europe and in East Asia), and from issue to issue (money vs. arms: obviously there should be no devolution of nuclear weaponry). But in all instances, our national interest will have to be seen as helping assure the compatibility of the different powers', or groupings of powers', *projets,* rather than providing them with the means (and sometimes even the régimes) for carrying out what remains, basically, our own *projet*. And insofar as world politics cannot any more be defined only as a contest of states, it will be in our interest to turn to the much-neglected community-building tasks, and to revive American idealism on their behalf. Thus, we will have to see ourselves again as one player among many, rather than as a specially-anointed missionary or teacher, and we will have to start looking at the world as a single planet, not merely from the viewpoint of promoting our cause or protecting our interests (while, needless to say, neither neglecting the latter, nor giving up the former).

This should help us turn our minds toward the two major difficulties such a switch will entail. The first is a new kind of contradiction: while there is an inherent instability in any attempt at indirect primacy, and while such an attempt inhibits community-building, devolution, and in particular the transfer of responsibilities to long-dependent clients and allies, may at first both multiply uncertainties, and make cacophony seem more probable than community. Interests repressed, situations kept frozen for many years, cannot be expected to adjust without trouble. Habits of reliance on the U.S., ingrained fears of responsibility and initiative, cannot be dispelled without pain. And yet, the more, in order to avoid such turbulence, we refrain from turning to this task, the more likely we make turbulence, pain and trouble once the inner contradictions and omissions of our present policy finally become unmanageable. In other words, in order to minimize instability and chaos, we have to engage others in long-range planning, concerted change and deliberate, well-defined emancipation, rather than in the confusing dialectic of surprise and reassurance.

The other difficulty is internal. If, as seems likely, the policy process becomes again less centralized, more splintered by checks and balances if domestic opinion and interests continue to assert themselves, will such a complex, discriminating and, in the short-run, apparently unrewarding approach to the national interest be at all possible? Won't it arouse both the opposition of all those, in the bureaucracy and the economy, who have acquired a stake in the preservation of the U.S. world system, and the criticisms of those who will discover that devolution and community-building do not mean an end of commitment and involvement, but a change in the kinds of entanglements and obligations? Will the political system be capable of the continuity, patience and flexibility required? If the answer is no, it is not only my own preferred definition of the national interest that will prove worthless; it will also be any attempt at waging foreign policy intelligently. And so, we are led back to an essential problem which underlies all speculations about the future role of the U.S. in world affairs: that of the aptitude of American society in general, and political elites in particular, to square two circles that no other great power ever had to square before—conducting an able foreign policy, at a time that is neither war nor Cold War, in accordance with democratic processes—and being far-sighted enough to transform a system of primacy, not because one's back is pressed to the wall, but because it appears to be the most sensible way of preserving one's own influence and of building a "stable structure of peace" in a troubled but single world.

Stanley Hoffmann is Professor of Government, Harvard University.

National Security for Whom?

Richard J. Barnet

From the smallest banana republic to the mightiest nuclear power, men who run governments like to invoke the magic words "national security." In the Soviet Union poets and historians are sent to Siberia in the name of national security. In Greece and Brazil anyone with a thirst for freedom or a developed sense of justice runs the risk of being tortured in the name of national security. And, in the United States in recent months, we have been confronted with a pattern of criminal conduct at the top of our government—spying, break-ins, secret wars, sabotage, provocations, systematic lying to the public and the elaborate mystification of the Congress—all justified by various participants in these activities, including, in more than one instance, the President of the United States, in the name of national security.

When it comes to distant countries and other ages all of us are remarkably prescient in detecting the self-serving and personal uses to which rulers put these familiar magic words. Schoolboys learn that kings regularly invented foreign threats against which they could make war, usually for the purpose of replenishing their treasuries and disposing of troublesome domestic opponents. Every student of the twentieth century knows how Stalin used the threat of "capitalist encirclement" to crush any possible rival at home and to tighten his dictatorial rule.

But it is now time to understand h

national security has been used to

alterations in the American system.

The presidential plumbers, the bug

propaganda and espionage teams unleas\

sition party are natural products of \

irrational fear that has been systematicall\   ꜳy

those in charge of defining and defen\   ₅ national

security over the last thirty years. Large bureaucracies

thrive comfortably on paranoia—Hanoi organized the

peace marchers; the Russians, the Cubans, or whoever,

financed the Democratic candidate. It is the same world

of self-serving make-believe that sustains our mammoth,

still growing, nuclear stockpile. Although 100 nuclear

weapons will destroy 50 per cent of the Soviet Union, the

Russians, despite their recent hospitality to Pepsi-Cola

and the Holiday Inn, are still considered too depraved to

be deterred by 8,000. Bureaucracies are quick to embrace

paranoid fantasies because they justify the accumulation

and the use of unlimited power.

A world in which all dangers are possible is a world

in which all means of defense are permitted. Quite

obviously, the graver the threat to national security the

higher the budget of the national security establishment,

the more generals, admirals, and militarized civilians will

be needed and the more impatient they have a right to be

with the clumsy processes of democracy. Watergate,

which is a code word for the use of the intelligence

underworld against the American political process itself,

was inevitable once two key assumptions about national

security became part of the political consensus.

First, the widely-accepted belief that protecting the

nation requires the national security establishment to

carry out most of its operations in secret has made this

the golden age of the official lie. Our failure as a nation

to understand that state secrets are always better known

abroad than at home has put us at the mercy of the secret

ors. (Readers of *Le Monde,* not to mention officials
the Kremlin, found few surprises in the Pentagon
Papers.)

Second, the atomic age truism that the President
must be able to act fast and alone to protect our interests
means that we usually do not have time even to find out
what those interests are. Together these assumptions
guarantee that the process of determining what national
security is and how it should be defined will be cut off
from all but a tiny fraction of the population. Without
effective checks, without even the restraint that probable
disclosure might impose, the President and his national
security advisors have felt free to use almost any means
against almost anyone—in the name of national security.
Is it really surprising that the same thug methods,
employed in some cases by the very same people, should
first be used against "external threats," such as Castro,
then the radicals of our own society, the Black Panthers,
the militant antiwar groups, and finally the opposition
party itself? (The logic of this inexorable process has also
produced an enemy list of Republicans.)

What we ought to learn from the events of the last
few years is that national security is such a sufficiently
slippery concept that it is commonly used to buttress
personal and bureaucratic power. It is frequently the case
that what is good for the Air Force or the CIA or
Kennecott Copper is not necessarily good for most
Americans. When the president of ITT and the former
director of the CIA, later on his payroll, declare that the
national security of the United States demands the
forcible overthrow of the Allende government in Chile,
the sincerity of such responsible figures must not be
doubted, but it does not mean that they have correctly
assessed the interests of 200 million Americans. Similarly,
every Air Force general who sees the "moral decay" of
the United States following in the wake of a bombing
halt in Cambodia, or every admiral who sees America's

geopolitical destiny tied to the racist régimes of Southern Africa, is also probably sincere, but their parochial views of the national interest do not necessarily reflect the real threats confronting this nation. Like individuals, societies survive by being able to adapt to changing circumstances. Those that are rooted in the reality of their time have a chance to survive. Those that are blinded by irrational fears do not. This convocation has met not to rake over the coals of the past but to explore some guidelines for the future. For the urgent task of redefining national security the first question that ought to concern us is this: Of what should we be afraid?

In any catalogue of threats the danger of physical attack is the most obvious. During the Cold War years the United States has spent substantially over $1.5 trillion to counter this danger on the assumption that its source was the Soviet Army, Navy, and Air Force (and what for many years were thought to be their Chinese allies). In these same years physical security in the United States has seriously deteriorated. The chances that you will be mugged in the street, hijacked in an airplane, or killed in your home have increased. Feelings of physical insecurity, as attested to by the thriving business in triple locks, pocket mace sprays, closed circuit television surveillance, formidable dogs, and private security forces, have mounted.

At the same time, President Nixon has downgraded the Soviet and Chinese threats, for which, I believe, we should all be grateful. Chou En-lai has been converted from a kind of Dr. No to a high-minded oriental statesman and Brezhnev is no longer a master of deceit but a man to do business with. None of these dramatic transformations of image mean that either China or Russia has less capacity to do us physical harm. Quite the contrary. The military might of the Soviet Union has never been greater. What has happened is that the foreign military threats have been redefined to a manageable level. During the Cold War it was the hope of four administrations that the overwhelming accumulation of U.S. military power at the edges of what was called the Sino-Soviet bloc would eventually bring an end to communist power in those countries. In the Dulles-Rusk era it was American dogma that people in this country could not ultimately be safe as long as communists controlled the governments in Moscow and Peking. Because the cost of trying to overturn the Russian and Chinese revolutions proved prohibitive, the U.S. has now settled for a more modest definition of national security. But most of the changes in U.S.-Soviet relations, it should be emphasized, took place in Washington, not Moscow. The "mellowing process" which was supposed to be the result of surrounding the mightiest land masses in the world with nuclear weapons has, much like "peace with honor" in Vietnam, been simply stipulated.

I mention all this to emphasize how *subjective* judgments about national security threats really are—and how quickly those judgments can change. Like the generals who built the Maginot Line, we continue to arm against obsolete and remote threats while more immediate dangers threaten to engulf us. Domestic and foreign security threats need to be seen not as rivals for attention but as part of a continuum. For most Americans it is now the air and streets of their own cities, not the Soviet ICBMs, which pose the daily threat to their health and safety. Of course, in a world of nuclear weapons we must maintain some deterrent force. But the issue is not so much the past, i.e., what do we do with our stockpiles, but the future. On what do we spend our money and our energy to get physical security in the remainder of the decade? The answer seems clear to me: we must spend it on trying to create a very different atmosphere in the United States. The question is not, as it was often put in the last presidential campaign: Do we have enough resources to defend our security and to rebuild our cities, house, feed, and educate our people, and clean our air and water at the same time? The fact is that unless this country can organize itself for a massive social reconstruction at home there will be no security for Americans.

There are many theories on what produces the pervasive spirit of lawlessness and cynicism in the United States: lawless and cynical government, for one. Perhaps most important is the insistent feeling in this country that neither Big Government nor Big Business cares about where most people live, about whether they have a job they can stand, or even a job at all, about whether they have enough money to raise a family, about whether they have a decent education or adequate medical care or a place in which to be taken care of when they are old. The problem of maintaining domestic tranquility in the United States is not a military problem or a matter of getting more police and better prisons. It is the political problem of resuming once again the historical process of building an American community. To do it requires facing the tough issues we have preferred to ignore or to ridicule: How do we revitalize the institutions of democracy so that the setting of national priorities is not the private preserve of the managers of our largest corporations and top national security bureaucrats? What new institutions do we need in the neighborhood, in the workplace, in the national government, to be able to carry forward the American experiment? How do we attack the threat to the personal security of every one of us that we have built in the name of national security? More specifically, how do we break down the walls that permit government bureaucrats and corporation executives to plan our future in secret? The exercise of concentrated and irresponsible power over the affairs of this nation is our greatest national security problem. The threat of tyranny in the United States is real, not a tyranny imposed from Russia, China, or Cuba, but homegrown in American soil. And in an atmosphere in which government rules through spies, provocateurs, informers, and saboteurs (the use of all of which has been admitted in recent weeks), no one is safe.

The second classic threat to national security is economic collapse. Throughout history wars have been fought to keep access routes open to the vital natural resources on which a national economy depends. America's five-ocean navy and vast military presence around the world has, as one of its primary functions, the continuation of the smooth flow of natural resources from virtually all parts of the globe. This nation consumes about forty per cent of the consumable resources each year. Were they to be cut off, the American "way of life" would pass into memory. (Motorists have already had a hint of this as they pulled up to empty gas stations.)

Thus, presumably, it is unsentimental self-interest that requires us to embrace the undemocratic regimes of Greece, Iran, Brazil, South Africa and their like. These governments are not "perfect," as State Department spokesmen will sometimes concede in "backgrounders," but they all allow access to their raw materials under reasonably favorable terms and, because of their own military power and ties with the United States, they have a healthy influence on any neighbors who might be tempted to pursue a more nationalistic course. The United States has believed for many years that internal changes within key countries in Latin America, certain parts of Africa and the Middle East, and in Southeast Asia had to be prevented with military power, if necessary, in the interests of national security. The result has been damaging to our own economic strength. The extraordinary accumulated military expense, particularly that of the Indochina war, has weakened the dollar, exhausted our gold reserves, and shattered world confidence in the leadership of the United States. In the process of defending our access to natural resources we have squandered much of what we have. With our heavy emphasis on military technology we have fallen far behind other nations of the world in producing and selling goods that people need or want for their daily lives. Today, the United States is rapidly becoming a service economy with more and more production of basic goods—shoes, textiles, automobiles, electronics—moving beyond our shores. The U.S. economy is becoming increasingly vulnerable to the decisions of foreigners, not because of the machinations of the Russians, but because of what we have done to ourselves.

Just as in the area of physical security, self-serving, parochial bureaucracies have distorted the national interest, so, in the area of economic policy, global corporations have pursued their own interests at the expense of the nation's strength and health. "I have long dreamed of buying an island owned by no nation and of establishing the World Headquarters of the Dow Company on the truly neutral ground of such an island, beholden to no nation or society," said Carl A. Gerstacker, chairman of the Dow Chemical Company. To transcend all nations, including this one, is the dream of the global corporation. Internationalism is a noble vision and nationalism a mean and inadequate response. But we have to look in quite specific terms at the effect on our society when our biggest economic units disclaim loyalty to the territory of the United States and deny responsibility for the problems which they help to create. Thomas Jefferson once observed, "Merchants have no country of their own. Their loyalty," he said, "is not to the land where they stand but to the land where they derive their gain." The same point occurred to President Eisenhower. "Capital is a curious thing," he told a Rio de Janeiro audience in 1960, "with perhaps no nationality. It flows where it is served best." The mobility of capital and technology now makes it possible to divide and shift tasks around the world in such a way as to maximize the world-wide profits of the global corporation—but often at the expense of individual countries including the United States. It is rational from the corporation's point of view to move its production out of the United States in order to pay thirty cents an hour in Singapore or fourteen cents an hour in Taiwan, rather than $3.40 in Massachusetts. But closed factories in the United States mean American workers out of jobs. As long as global corporations have the right to move in and out of the United States at will, without responsibility for their impact on employment, they constitute a continuing threat to national security.

There are other areas, too, where the very mobility of global corporations makes it impossible for the government of the U.S. to effectively govern American territory. As Andrew Brimmer of the Federal Reserve Board recently pointed out, the activities of multinational companies and banks "in mobilizing and re-channeling funds" have made the U.S. more open to "foreign financial developments." Global corporations have been speculating against the dollar and have contributed to the weakness of our currency. Unlike citizens who live in the territory of the United States, corporations can minimize the risk of currency fluctuations by buying up several different currencies. Corporations escape taxes by means of their foreign operations and thus contribute to the deepening fiscal crisis in the United States, which makes it impossible for the world's richest nation to afford its citizens a level of social services ordinarily available in the middle-sized countries of Western Europe.

With a military force "second to none," as our presidents keep proclaiming, we have a record in health care, pollution control, social security, and enlightened employment policies that compares unfavorably with many other industrialized societies. By making ordinary business decisions, the managers of firms like GM, IBM,

GE, Pfizer, General Foods, Shell, and Pepsico now have more power than most sovereign governments—including, in many areas, the government of the United States—to determine where people live, what work if any they will do, what they will eat, drink, and wear, what sort of knowledge schools and universities will encourage, and what kind of society their children will inherit. There is abundant evidence that, in making these decisions, the global balance sheet—not the interests of the American people or those of any other nation—is the guiding star. Unfortunately, there is increasing conflict between what makes global corporations feel secure and what offers security for the rest of us who must stay at home.

The concentrated power in the hands of national security bureaucrats and corporate statesmen has prevented us from even recognizing, much less confronting, our real security problems as a nation. We cannot build an American community that can offer personal freedom and individual security merely by attacking the Pentagon and IBM. Our security problems are not automatically solved by breaking the power of these self-serving bureaucracies to define the American purpose. But a redistribution of power within this country is an absolute precondition for realizing individual and community security in America.

Once we have the political space and the moral courage to come to terms with our age, we can begin to develop an alternative vision of world politics that can offer real security. There is today no national security except in the context of a system of global security. The American people cannot find security in a world in which most people are subsisting on less than $300 a year. It is not merely a matter of having one's dinner disturbed by watching hungry children with swollen bellies appear on the TV screen. The relatively rich and comfortable are increasingly vulnerable to "monkey wrench politics," the ability of the weak and powerless to make life unpleasant through hijackings, sabotage, kidnappings, etc. Moreover, the isolationism inherent in our traditional policy of trying to make the world safe for the United States through military power represents so mean a vision that it can neither inspire nor unite us—particularly since even the inspiration of anti-communism is now gone. If security is defined as merely holding on to what we have by holding back the tides of humanity beyond our shores, we will never recover the spiritual health and political confidence that are the prerequisites of real strength. President Nixon and his foreign policy advisers are quite correct when they declare that only a confident and buoyant nation can make a positive contribution to building a system of international security. But they are wrong when they think that exhortations to positive thinking or the pretense that national scandals do not exist will provide that confidence. Nations, like individuals, begin to develop confidence when they are realizing their full potential.

Indeed, the only real security is in development. In terms of its potential to solve its own social problems by the rational use of its extraordinary resources, in terms of its possibilities for helping to reduce misery in the world, particularly by abandoning those of its own policies which increase it, such as the international arms traffic, the United States is an underdeveloped country. We could show the world that the first requirement of being "developed" is ecological security—being at peace with nature instead of at war. We could show the world that physical security is found by demilitarization, not militarism. But we continue to preach precisely the opposite messages and it is these messages on which so-called practical statesmen in every country base their actions. Were the United States, which is still the model of development around the world, to demonstrate that it could solve, or even that it was interested in solving, the three great political problems of the twentieth century—

mass poverty, mass unemployment and social uselessness of men and women, and the staggering inequalities of wealth and power that destroy political community—the effect would be electric across the whole planet.

There is nothing easy about development. If the United States were truly prepared to search for an alternative vision of a global security—not *Pax Americana* with profile high or low, nor a cynical partnership of thermonuclear giants, we would have to pose some very tough questions to ourselves. If we cannot make the world safe for the United States, how do we make the United States safe for the world? Specifically, how do we change patterns of consumption in this country so that we do not continue to use an obscenely disproportionate share of the world's resources? How do we develop the confidence at home so that we can dare to relax our grip on the underdeveloped world and permit a variety of experimental approaches to development which the poorest countries so desperately need? Finally, how do we work towards the orderly redistribution of power in the world and the vesting of vital decisions in the hands of those who are most affected by them? The world has two seemingly contradictory needs: a coherent global vision of how the human community might be organized, and a decentralization of power. Their reconciliation represents the most extraordinary challenge to man's political ingenuity in all human history. But if we do not rise to meet it, there will be no security for anyone.

Richard J. Barnet is Co-founder and Co-director of the Institute for Policy Studies and a former official of the U.S. Arms Control & Disarmament Agency.

The Need for a More Modest Role

Robert W. Tucker

How are the national interests of the United States currently defined? On balance, they are defined today in much the same way as they were defined in the recent past. Whatever the hopes of some and the fears of others, in the aftermath of Vietnam, the essential structure of the nation's post World War II interests and commitments has been preserved; the elements of continuity in America's world role predominate over the elements of change.

This conclusion can scarcely be deemed a revelation. It was foreseeable in the very debate over foreign policy that the war in Vietnam precipitated. For the principal thrust of the criticism of American policy that the war provoked was directed less to the basic conceptions of role and interest that have defined policy since World War II than to the nature of the world in which the nation's role and interests were to be preserved. Despite interpretations to the contrary, the prevailing criticism of the late 1960s did not so much signal a basic break from the foreign policy consensus as it did an insistence upon readjusting that consensus to changing circumstances abroad and at home. The Nixon Administration, though resisting its critics on Vietnam, responded to the larger debate occasioned by Vietnam by assimilating—indeed, by claiming as its own discovery—most of the major points that by 1968 had come to represent conventional criticism.

Thus the new Administration adopted the view that the conditions marking the period of the classic Cold War had been profoundly altered and that American policy must adjust to a changed world. More pointedly, it decried an outlook and style marked by unlimited aspirations and unmindful of what American power could reasonably accomplish. It called for a new modesty in thought and action by emphasizing the inherent limits to any nation's wisdom, understanding, and energy. It abandoned anti-communism as a guiding principle. Instead, its cool tone suggested that crusades of any kind were the very antithesis of the new style and outlook. At the same time, it did not relinquish the substance of interest, but promised change in the methods by which interest would henceforth be served. Even in Asia, the emphasis throughout has been on method. Although promising no more Vietnams, the Nixon Administration has not conceded that the price might be a substantial sacrifice of American interests.

This is not to say that the Nixon Doctrine has precluded any change in the structure of American interests. Though the emphasis has been on style and method, the Administration has conceded from the start that a changed world also permitted and even required a certain redefinition of interests. In an increasingly pluralistic world, the domino theory must at least be modified, but so also must the interest one has in each and every domino. Since pluralism implies that there is no "test case" for wars of national liberation, the interest in intervening in any particular war of national liberation is subject to change. If the process of modernization is going to prove to be slow and painful, and its course cannot be controlled by outsiders, there is no need to see in it a matter of vital concern. If China is no longer found capable of or intent upon overturning the Asian balance of power, the interest in containing China may be reinterpreted. They were once among the commonplaces of conventional criticism—that change was required not only in the methods but in the interests of policy. They are also among the recognizable features of the present Administration's philosophy and—to an as yet uncertain degree—policy.

Yet a redefinition of interests, contingent upon a cautiously optimistic view of the world, does not add up to an historic turning point in American foreign policy. Innovations in diplomatic method aside, the change in role and interests foreshadowed by the Nixon Doctrine— and realized, to date, in policy—has been of modest proportion. In the new world, America would still play a predominant role and American power would still remain the indispensable element in fashioning a "stable and lasting structure of peace." This order would no longer be defined primarily—if, indeed, at all—in ideological terms. Instead, the requirements of order would increasingly be defined in the traditional idiom of diplomacy. More generally, the detailed requirements of the order sought by this nation would remain relaxed, though the extent of this relaxation would remain unclear in doctrine and, in any event, would have to be seriously tested in practice. But these qualifications do not substantially invalidate the point that for this Administration, as for its predecessors, the nation's security and well-being would continue to be broadly equated with a world in which America occupies a preponderant position in the international hierarchy and in which change could be effected only in certain ways, while certain types of change would be precluded altogether.

In a period of domestic pressures for retrenchment and détente, the guiding assumption of the Nixon policy reformulation has been that the U.S. can maintain its predominant position in the world but at a lower and domestically tolerable price. On the theory that major allies have nowhere else to go—and, even more importantly perhaps, no will to go anywhere—they can be pressured to compromise on a range of economic and security issues. While deterred from challenging America's military hegemony over them, an hegemony the Nixon Administration has shown no desire to relinquish in its quest for "more balanced and equal partnerships," this nation will presumably enjoy the freedom of maneuver and independence of action necessary to broaden a détente with its adversaries. Thus while maintaining a holding operation with respect to allies, the triangular relationship will be developed in which America holds the initiative if only by virtue of its role as "balancer" between the great communist powers. And if the more grandiose aspirations of yesterday must be set aside and equilibrium and stability acknowledged as the central goals of policy, there is the satisfaction that America remains the principal guarantor of a global order now openly and without equivocation identified with the *status quo.*

Although the Nixon policy reformulation has elicited its share of criticism, the main thrust of this criticism does not reveal a breakdown in the foreign policy consensus of the past generation. A small minority apart, the debate occasioned by the new foreign policy— Vietnam always excepted—has been very much an in-house debate carried on within implicitly well-defined limits. Certainly, this debate shows little disposition to question the fundamental assumption that equates the nation's security with maintenance of the essential postwar structure of American interests and commitments. On the contrary, that assumption is reaffirmed in the emphasis most critics have placed on the need to preserve and even to strengthen our principal alliances. Indeed, the charge most commonly brought against the Nixon foreign policy has been its presumed willingness to buy political advantage at home and détente abroad at the price of allied solidarity. Implicit in this very charge, however, is a rejection of any serious effort to change the

structure of American interests and commitments. Disagreements over method and even over priorities, though
sharp on occasion, are not to be confused with disagreements over the substance of America's role in the world.
That role can be significantly altered only through a
far-reaching devolution of power and responsibility. But
such devolution must in turn entail nuclear proliferation
and loss of American influence, consequences both the
Administration and its critics consider inimical to vital
American interests.

Is the persisting view that equates our security with
our principal postwar interests and commitments any
longer persuasive or even plausible? It would not seem so.
Certainly, it would not seem so if by security we mean
primarily the physical security of the U.S. Whereas only a
generation ago it was reasonable to see America's
security, including her physical security, largely in terms
of conventional balance-of-power calculations, today that
view is no longer reasonable. Whereas a generation ago it
was plausible to find in alliances an indispensable hedge
against an uncertain future, today the indispensability of
alliances is no longer plausible. The principal reason for
this change—this radical change—in the conditions of
American security is clear enough. For the state that can
now destroy any other state or combination of states,
nuclear weapons have conferred what has heretofore
proven unachievable—a surfeit of deterrent power.

It is indeed the case that in the extreme situation
the great nuclear power is absolutely vulnerable with
respect to its great adversary. But this ultimate vulnerability cannot be significantly reduced—let alone
removed—by any alliance the great nuclear power may
form—or retain. In other than the extreme situation,
nuclear weapons confer a degree of security on their
principal possessors that great powers seldom, if ever,
enjoyed in the past. Provided that America maintains the
strategic forces necessary to deter attack, alliances cannot
enhance a physical security that is no longer dependent

on what transpires outside the North American continent.

If retention of the postwar system of commitments is to be justified in terms of a narrow concept of security, the grounds for doing so must be other than conventional balance-of-power calculations. Can these grounds be found in the nuclear proliferation that would presumably attend a substantial contraction of American commitments? There is no gainsaying the argument that, all other things being equal, the greater the number of states possessing nuclear weapons the greater the chances of a nuclear conflict. States that do not have nuclear weapons cannot be tempted to use them. The relevant question here, however, is not whether nuclear proliferation increases in some measure the chances of nuclear conflict, but whether this increase is such as to have any practical significance for America's security.

The answer to this question depends upon the assumptions that are made about the character of American security interests and, more generally, the nature of a nuclear peace. If it is assumed that America retains unchanged her present interests, then proliferation is indeed likely to increase the danger of America becoming involved in nuclear conflict. But this assumption establishes a vital American security interest in non-proliferation only by begging the question of how her vital security interests should be defined. If the assumption that America retains her present interests is not made, the threat to American security arising from further spread of nuclear weapons must depend very largely upon the argument that nuclear peace is indivisible.

The argument for an indivisible nuclear peace obviously cannot be based upon historical evidence. A nuclear peace may prove at least as divisible as any other peace men have known. Given the expected consequences of employing nuclear weapons, it may in fact prove even more divisible. Nor is it only the hazards of entering a nuclear war that may henceforth be expected to militate in favor of a divisible peace. Yesterday, peace was indivisible to the degree that an imbalance of military power was the possible (even the probable) price of choosing isolation from a conflict involving the other major states. Today, peace is divisible to the degree that a balance-of-deterrent power would be at worst unaffected and at best improved, by choosing isolation from a nuclear conflict involving the other major nuclear powers.

In a system governed by a conventional balance of power, the fear of being isolated was, with rare exception, synonymous with the fear of vulnerability to attack by superior forces. Thus, the conclusion was drawn, and hardened into dogma, that peace is indivisible, that the principal military powers must all be at peace or all at war. In a system governed by a balance-of-deterrent nuclear power, however, the fears of isolation and vulnerability to attack are no longer synonymous. To this extent, we must reverse what has come to be one of the received truths of the age, namely, that nuclear weapons have created a "community of fate." Instead, the effects of these weapons have been to make peace more divisible than it has been in a very long time.

Even when it is conceded that America's core security no longer depends upon retaining the postwar structure of commitments, we are reminded that great powers have seldom—if ever—restricted their interests to physical safety. We are also warned that we cannot "abandon" the world, in reaction to past attempts to "control" the world, without paying a very considerable—and, to many, even a prohibitive—price. Despite occasional dire prophecies to the contrary, there is little reason to fear an America that has "quit the world." At the same time, we ought to ask how dependent we are on our environment, if not in terms of physical security then in terms of material well-being and, more generally, the quality of life in America.

Before doing so, it may be useful to point out what should be apparent, but is no longer so. Dependence—

including reciprocal dependence or interdependence—is not by definition a desirable condition. It is so only to the extent it facilitates desired goals that could not be achieved—or that would prove far more difficult to achieve—in the absence of interdependency. Those who stress the inescapability of interdependence are evidently describing what they believe to be an objective condition from which we can escape, if at all, only at a very exorbitant price. Frequently, however, they also assume the desirability *per se* of increasing interdependence, if only for the reason that interdependence will presumably bring us peace. But interdependence in a world where nation-states remain the effective centers of decision is not necessarily productive of peace (or, for that matter, of lesser goods). It is so only if we assume that by virtue of this interdependence the costs of pursuing an independent course of action—above all, of using armed force— have become prohibitive and that all parties comprising the emergent "global community" are aware of this. Yet there is no persuasive evidence that this is the case today. Even if it is acknowledged that the costs of using armed force have risen dramatically, at least for the major powers, the change must be found elsewhere than in interdependence.

Nor is this all. Far from being desirable, a greater measure of interdependence in a world where the triumph of the nation-state has been universalized may prove a considerable liability. This is all the more so to the extent armed force is increasingly at a discount for the major powers. In such a world, we must mortgage our future to an environment we have less prospect of controlling than great powers have normally enjoyed in the past. It may well be true that we have no real choice but to adjust to an environment over which we will have decreasing control. There is no apparent reason, however, why we should celebrate this prospect. There is still less reason why we should desire to develop interdependencies that may be avoided without serious injury to ourselves or to others.

The case for and against America's economic dependence on the world has been dealt with on so many occasions in recent years that it is redundant to repeat the by-now-familiar litany of arguments. At issue in this debate is not whether America's foreign economic involvement represents a significant interest. Few would care to deny that it does. What is at issue is how significant this involvement has become to the nation's continued material well-being and, whatever its precise significance, the means by which it may best be preserved.

At the very least, one is entitled to view skeptically the position that the American economy could not function as presently constituted without our foreign economic interests. Scenarios based on the assumption that imports to the U.S. were suddenly cut off and overseas investments just as suddenly expropriated give this position a semblance of plausibility. Even if the assumption is granted, there is room for debate over the effects. Many believe that, far from collapsing, the American economy would adapt, though standards of living would suffer a modest decline. At any rate, the assumption on which such speculation is based appears wildly improbable, short of a global conflict in which the sudden sacrifice of our foreign economic interests is likely to be among the least of the catastrophes besetting the nation. A more reasonable, though still highly improbable scenario, would allow for a period of time in which to make the necessary adjustments to the loss of imports and of foreign investments. And, given a period of time, there are no persuasive reasons for assuming that the American economy could not adjust remarkably well to the changes required.

Even if the presumed dependence of the economy on the foreign sector were accepted as a fact, it does not follow that there is a necessary relationship between this fact and the maintenance of military-strategic interests that have largely defined the American role in the world since the 1940s. At least it does not follow unless one assumes that the preservation of our foreign economic interests is in turn dependent upon preserving the structure of America's political-military commitments. Yet that assumption is now seldom avowed, particularly with respect to the nations comprising the third world. Instead, it is commonly argued that what threat there is at present to America's interests in the developing states is not likely to be turned away by persisting in a policy of alliance and intervention. Significantly, the rejection of military intervention, or the threat of such intervention, is extended to the case of Middle Eastern oil on the grounds that even here the costs of pursuing an interventionist policy would outweigh any reasonable expectation of benefits.

It is with respect to the developed nations that a relationship is still drawn between the preservation of our foreign economic interests and the maintenance of alliance commitments. Clearly, these interests would be placed in jeopardy if one were to assume the control of Western Europe and Japan by hostile powers. This altogether improbable contingency apart, the effectiveness of using our alliances as a lever to preserve economic interests or to extract short-term economic advantage is increasingly open to question. Nothing seems more likely to engender lasting resentments than the attempt to employ our military hegemony to these ends. Nor does anything seem more likely in the long run to endanger our economic interests with the developed states than a growing conviction that those interests rest upon military superiority rather than upon mutual economic advantage.

It is neither our physical security nor our material well-being that precludes a substantial modification of, even a radical change in, the global role we continue to play, but the prospect of a world in which American influence, though still considerable, would markedly decline. It is this prospect of a reduced American role that successive administrations have insistently identified as a threat to the nation's security. The determination not to lose America's preponderant position in the world continues almost undiminished today, despite the novel methods employed of late to preserve this preponderance. Novel methods aside, however, the reluctance to accept a more modest role largely accounts for opposition to a serious reappraisal of our alliance relationships. The same reluctance largely accounts for the devotion to "partnerships" without equality, "regionalism" without dominant regional powers, and "change" without instability.

If the preceding considerations have merit, the issue of defining our national interests today must be seen to turn for the most part on intangible considerations. To say that these considerations are intangible is in no way to diminish their importance. The vision which a nation—or a nation's leadership—entertains of its role in history is no less crucial for being rooted in intangible considerations. Whether this nation can face up to abandoning the aspirations it has entertained and the role it has played since World War II without corrosive effects on its domestic life is by no means clear. Much would depend upon the manner and spirit in which the U.S. seeks to adjust to a more modest role. What does seem reasonably clear is that the attempt will have to be made in the not too distant future, since there is little reason for believing that present power structure—dependent as it largely is upon the prevention of further nuclear proliferation—can be sustained indefinitely. At the very least, this attempt ought not to be burdened by the appeal to interests that do not condition our physical safety and material well-being.

Robert W. Tucker is Professor of Political Science at The Johns Hopkins University.

IV

A SPECTRUM OF VIEWS
ON THE NATIONAL INTEREST

*The discussion of the national interest produced a broad
spectrum of foreign policy views. An opening attack took
Richard Barnet and Robert Tucker to task for lack of
emphasis on moral principles.*

George F. Will:

Mr. Barnet's answer to the central question before us, "Of what does the real interest of the United States consist?" is, I think, less arresting than his reduction of that question to another, "Of what should we be afraid?" As regards foreign policy, he seems to conceive of national interest simply as a matter of physical safety. His ideas regarding minimal deterrence and domestic reconstruction are extreme and extremely vague, but they are actually less extreme than the extent to which he has expunged from his concept of the national interest all traces of obligation for the United States to use its power for moral purposes beyond achieving physical security.

Mr. Tucker, I believe, tends toward this point of view, implicitly equating commendable modesty in foreign policy with a disinclination for crusades. I suspect that this reflects a highly dubious assumption that moralism in some way caused our Vietnam misadventure and that hence, a consciously moralistic foreign policy is imprudent. I assume Mr. Barnet shares Mr. Tucker's implied hope that the U.S. will come to occupy something less than a preponderant position in the world. But

I would suggest that if the current and foreseeable balance of strategic forces serves deterrence as well as both speakers assume it will, then economic power will continue to eclipse military power as the critical variable in international politics. And the United States, more clearly preponderant economically than militarily, will find its power, for good or ill, enhanced. Indeed, U.S. trading policy will almost *be* U.S. foreign policy.

That is why I, for one, believe that the greatest drama today is the struggle by Senator [Henry M.] Jackson to force the Administration to use our enormous trade leverage to extract a modicum of liberty from tyrannical régimes. His proposal represents a new way for the U.S. to conduct a peaceful and prudent foreign policy on behalf of humane values, a frankly moralistic policy, but without the reckless moralism that can accompany the use of military force. Our speakers do not address themselves to the axiom at the heart of the Jackson effort. That axiom is: in an age of government-directed and subsidized trade, which is to say, in an age of politicized trade policies, we shall inevitably make policy choices that have vast consequences. We shall not inevitably make virtuous choices. We certainly shall not make virtuous choices if we discuss the national interest without reference to our continuing interest in the humane values, to which the United States is and should remain dedicated at home and abroad.

George F. Will is Chief of the Washington bureau of The National Review.

Barnet:

I'm grateful to Mr. Will for calling my speech arresting, but I'm afraid it didn't stop him long enough to get one important point that I did make. And that is that the elements of security are not only physical security, protection from physical attacks, but also preservation from economic collapse and internal dissolution. The point of my remarks really was that a government pursuing a foreign policy by the means which we have used, risks the destruction of its own institutions, something which we have seen again and again throughout history. I believe that there are moral principles on which foreign policy needs to be based. I think that the matter of political prisoners and the treatment of dissidents or minorities is a terribly important universal problem. And I would have hoped that Senator Jackson, rather than limiting himself to a tragic situation in one area of the world, would have addressed himself to those areas of the world where, in fact, the United States has considerably more influence through AID programs and other means and where we encourage régimes which make it a practice to engage in far greater inroads on human liberty.

Specifically, I would like to see the United States stop its support for régimes that use torture as an instrument of policy and recognize that this is a problem which is now of increasing seriousness, across the political spectrum, in both left- and right-wing governments. And perhaps we should call a conference this year under the auspices of the United Nations and talk about the trend toward deterioration of human liberty all across the world. I think the United States ought to take the lead in that.

Harvey Wheeler:

I've been trying to sort out the meaning of the debate that's been taking place here over such matters as national interest and balance of power. It is now obvious that there is difficulty in identifying the players in the nation-state system and that the old kind of balance-of-power systems are no longer applicable. Thus let's see if we can identify some of these problems the way they come across to us.

First, as to national interest: I take it that it is certainly true that the national interest is real, but it seems to me that it is a useless definition except in the case of very broad issues, such as war and survival. On specific issues it seems useless as a test of policy. That has been illustrated here as every conceivable position has been advocated under the rubric of national interest. Of course, one can say that nobody advocates policies against the national interest. But the problem is that we only know what was in the national interest after the fact. That's one of the problems that we get into with the notion of national interest. It is the construct, basically, of historians. They can reconstruct events around an analysis of what was or must have been in the national interest and what was not in the national interest and describe history that way. But to use it as a reliable policy device in looking to the future, except for the very broadest issues, its application is a practical impossibility.

Next, as to the balance of power: true, balance-of-power politics is a permanent historical feature. Again, however, it is a permanent historical feature only considered broadly, because its nature changes and has changed with the nature of the change of the entities in the structures involved in the struggle. What is often talked about, and decried, under the term "balance of power" is a quite specific form of balance of power that was perfected in the nineteenth century. And it had special entities, namely, the nation-states. But we also know, and we've been told many times, that these entities are changing their forms, that they are becoming more permeable, and that national policies are less applicable. As that transition happens, so the nature of balance of power and balance-of-power struggle also changes. This change, of course, was realized in the Cold War. One way of describing the Cold War is as a form of relationship which the world successors to nation-states developed in order to find the way to deal with their relationships in a world where the nation-state system itself was dissolving. This is a more general and less ideological description of the Cold War than is normally used. As these changes take place, we are also witnessing a new kind of balance-of-power struggle. Here at *Pacem in Terris III* Senator Fulbright illustrated what seems to be a very dramatic application of this new balance-of-power struggle when he talked about the necessity for opposing the Jackson and Mondale measures. The reason he opposed those measures, he told us, was that he felt they would have a serious and perhaps disastrous effect upon the internal power struggles within the Soviet Union. That's the sort of thing I mean about the new balance-of-power problems. As we look around the world today, and as we look over the history of our foreign policy, we see the world and the history of that policy in terms of varying factions of hawks and doves that make up the power entities inside the nations concerned. We design our foreign policy—not entirely but in some good part—on the basis of the calculated effect it will have on the domestic power struggles taking place in other countries.

All can be very concretely illustrated by the Nixon-Kissinger overtures to Mao Tse-tung and Chou En-lai. Those were made almost explicitly in terms of the calculation that it would be possible to strengthen the powers of a more amicable faction inside China. Looking back a bit further, when Premier Khrushchev was designing his own responses to American overtures, he decided that he would release the American aviators who were being held in prison in Russia just prior to the American election, on the calculation, as he announced publicly afterward, that this would help influence the American election and would help John F. Kennedy into power. Now of course his calculation may have been wrong; he might have fared better had Kennedy not come into power. These illustrations can be multiplied indefinitely.

What I'm suggesting is that the structure in which international power relationships takes place is changing. And it is producing a new kind of informal network, a network in which policies are designed to influence the domestic balance of power inside other countries. This new form of balance-of-power struggle has a new kind of content. The old still exists, obviously, and is powerful; it deals with the traditional tools: economic power, one's resources, and so on. The new one, it seems to me, deals with what might be called a kind of "organizational geo-politics." We cannot understand and we cannot analyze the nature of the struggle that is taking place in the world today without bearing in mind the dualism of the continuation of the old balance-of-power struggle alongside the inauguration of a new form of it.

What we have been talking about here is the *demilitarization* of the old balance-of-power struggle. We are all certainly for that. But what must be borne in mind, if we are to appreciate and understand the new dual nature of the balance-of-power struggle, is that a large proportion of the troubles we've gotten into recently in the world have been because of the militarization of this new balance-of-power struggle. That's what happened in Vietnam and in other countries. So when we speak of demilitarization it seems to me that we must keep in mind both of these aspects of balance-of-power politics. We must not only demilitarize the traditional balance-of-power struggle, but also conduct this new balance-of-power struggle, as many people have suggested, although using different words, by endowing it with nobility and the grandeur, making our overtures in those terms, rather than covert invasion and the violation of other peoples' politics.

Harvey Wheeler is a Senior Fellow of the Center for the Study of Democratic Institutions.

Morgenthau:

First, let me say that the idea of the national interest is not an invention of particular pressure groups within a society, or of the government, but has an objective reality. Its content has been consistent over a long period of history. In a profound sense you can say that the American national interest has been identically identified from the time of the Founding Fathers to the present day.

Secondly, I disagree with the idea that has been expressed so frequently here: the notion that the balance of power is obsolete. To me, this is like saying that the law of gravity has become obsolete. You may refer to the balance of power as it exists at present with a different terminology from that used in the past, but that is only to say that previous manifestations of the balance of power are different from what they are today.

Mr. Wheeler, for example, has spoken of a new balance of power dealing with internal distribution of power within different countries. There's nothing new about this at all. In the nineteenth century the Russians used to buy control of French newspapers for their own purposes, to put pressure on the French government in favor of their own policies. And the Italian papers, with very few exceptions, were ready to be sold to the highest bidder for foreign political purposes. I cannot see how one can deny that our relations with the Soviet Union since the end of the second World War have been based on the same balance-of-power principles you find in Thucydides' record of the Peloponnesian Wars.

Against the overriding characteristic of our age, of our thinking and acting with regard to foreign policy, is the discrepancy between the objective conditions under which we live and the modes of thought and action with which we approach those conditions. We think and act as though nothing drastic has happened since the end of the second World War, while in truth the human condition, not to speak of the national condition, has been transformed almost beyond recognition. This is most obvious in the field of nuclear matters where the whole obsolete series of thoughts and actions, from defense through nuclear arms races, through proliferation, really deal with the concepts which were perfectly appropriate fifty years ago, or 2,000 years ago, but which have been rendered obsolete by the availability of nuclear weapons.

My main criticism of the foreign policy of the present Administration, with much of which I happen to agree, is that the Administration uses one word to define its conception of the future: stability. Unfortunately, in large areas of the world—you may safely say in most of the world—there reigns profound instability. And you cannot create stability out of instability without having corrected the objective conditions out of which instability has arisen. In other words, most of the world lives in a pre-revolutionary or evolutionary condition. And yet we try to superimpose upon this condition an order which, in my view, is going to be swept away by revolutionary upheavals throughout the world. This was the fate of Metternich's policy, and it is likely to be the fate of its epigones.

Finally, one cannot conceive of an effective, I would even say a decent, American foreign policy without taking the ethos of America into account, as it reveals itself, in domestic affairs. Again, this is not a new discovery. This is not a new phenomenon. This was as true at the beginning of the Republic 200 years ago as it is today. And I believe that it is a peculiarity of the United States that its effectiveness in the world is profoundly and organically connected with its domestic decencies and the domestic picture it presents to its own people as well as to the rest of the world. Throughout our history we have offered ourselves to the world as an example to emulate. And what is more important, the rest of the world, by and large, has accepted that self-image which America has formed of itself. But today America offers the world not something to emulate but something to avoid. Consequently our foreign policy has lost that impetus, that dynamism, that plausibility which it had before. Thus, without the restoration of that traditional American ethos, there cannot be, in my view, an effective American foreign policy.

Stanley Karnow:

I'd like to speak about the interrelationship of foreign policy and domestic considerations. I'm inclined to agree with Robert Tucker that continuity rather than change characterizes American foreign policy. Moreover, it seems to me the Nixon Administration is striving to perpetuate American predominance in the world, even though, as Stanley Hoffmann pointed out, its quest for primacy may be indirect. But I think I may be more alarmed by the prospect of increasing tensions, both within this country and in its relationships abroad if we are unable to adapt to the fact that this is not the American century, but a period in which the big powers as well as the smaller nations have to work out a realistic pattern of interdependence. We have become increasingly dependent on each other.

The notion that the United States is the global leader can be seen in the Administration's lobbying for a large defense budget, its calling for more sophisticated weapons. It can also be seen, as Richard Barnet points out, in the President's fixation on national security as a device to broaden his authority and his repeated warnings that an overwhelmingly powerful America is the only guarantee of peace. The Nixon doctrine, as I interpret it, appears to be a further effort to assure a *Pax Americana* under a new and perhaps less costly guise.

Professor Hoffmann spoke of the "redistribution of burdens." I think it's a good term. Although the concept has been publicized to mean a more subdued American presence overseas, it plainly states that the United States will honor its commitments to help other countries to resist communism. And therefore it signifies a continuous military activity abroad, in one form or another. I'm reminded of a phrase used to describe the American doctrine by a senior official who jokingly said, "We're lowering our profile, while keeping our end up."

Thus, the Administration bitterly fights for continuation of the bombing in Cambodia and when that fails it pledges to provide all possible economic and military support to the Lon Nol regime. At the same time, it is providing, or trying to get, two and a half billion dollars in military and economic aid for South Vietnam. And it maintains bases in Thailand in order to exert influence in future events in Indochina. But with all this it seems to me that in the years ahead the United States is going to be compelled by interrelated circumstances to accept a more modest role in the world. On the one hand, we're going to face double-barreled economic pressures abroad, both from competitive industrial states like Japan and the countries in Western Europe, and the raw material-producing nations of what we call the third world. I think we're already witnessing the power of the "impotent," as the Arab states use their oil as a political weapon. And the day may not be far off when we are pitted against the Japanese and Europeans in an attempt to win over the Middle East oil resources. If Brezhnev considers détente to be only a tactic, as he said recently, we may expect our quest for resources to be complicated by Soviet maneuvers.

On the domestic front, meanwhile, the curbing of our industrial capacity, caused by a lack of energy and other shortages, could have serious repercussions. Mr. Barnet referred to the motorists lining up to get gasoline. When we have trouble getting gasoline on Thursdays as well as Sundays, we may begin to link our domestic plight to our international posture. It seems to me unlikely, even if conditions worsen, however, that Americans will favor sending gunboats against either our competitors or suppliers. Yet, despite this, we strangely cling to the idea of military power as the key to our security.

At the risk of sounding overly pessimistic, I find it difficult to imagine that Americans will accept the reality of a more modest United States, a more modest American position abroad until they have experienced a domestic crisis related to an excess of American ambition abroad. Vietnam was a step in that direction, but I think its effects were less than pervasive. Environmental, food, energy and monetary problems may have a greater impact. Mr. Tucker said correctly that the diplomatic innovations of this Administration do not add up an historic turning-point in American foreign policy. But historic turning-points do not occur overnight. I think we are going through a turning-point that we may not fully recognize at this time. In my view a crunch will come when we finally realize that America's great aspiration, the sense of Manifest Destiny that began around the turn of the century, cannot be fulfilled. And only then, I believe, will we start to adjust more gracefully to more plausible goals.

Stanley Karnow is a Contributing Editor of The New Republic.

Leslie Gelb:

A new reasonableness is sweeping the intellectual parlors of the United States. It has two mutually consistent and reinforcing voices. One is the voice of logic arguing that the remoteness of threats in nuclear deterrence now allow and behoove us to define U.S. national interests in terms of the divisibility of peace. That's Mr.

Tucker's view. The other is the voice of domestic priorities and compassion, pleading that peace begins at home and that security lies in development. That's Mr. Barnet's opinion. I, too, am caught up by this new reasonableness, except when I'm reminded of the old. It was not long ago when political leaders, the intellectual community, and the news media had other fashions in sweet reason. Then, we could see little wrong with concepts like the indivisibility of peace and the necessity of having and keeping commitments, of having the military capability for "flexible and controlled response." As Tallulah Bankhead said when the bride and groom marched down the aisle, "I've had them both and they were awful."

Some can adjust with remarkable ease and speed from one absolute certainty to the next. I cannot. Vietnam stands in the way. It has caused me to lose confidence in my judgment in matters of great moment such as defining the national interest of the United States. For many, Vietnam served as a springboard from the past to new truths. For me, it has become a roadblock against embracing even the nicest of verities. Vietnam transformed most of the right-thinking people from prophets of the Old Testament to apostles of the New Testament. Vietnam has left me an agnostic about America's future interests. This of course makes me unfit to offer answers. I can only wonder.

I wonder if the best way to help the dissidents in the Soviet Union is to risk détente and deny Moscow certain economic benefits until its policy is revised, or to grant those economic benefits as a means to extract a concession, later. Unlike Mr. Tucker, I believe it is in our interest to prevent the spread of nuclear weapons, but I wonder about the best way of doing this. I believe that our military presence helps to keep the peace in Europe, and even in Korea, but I wonder how many of our forces should be withdrawn from this theater, and when. How do we weigh the claims of the Israelis versus the

Palestinians? Is it right ethically or practically to stay out of the Middle East? Is human dignity any more precious in the Soviet Union or China than it is in Greece or South Vietnam? I wonder about the surprises of history, the changes in the leadership of nations that can so readily turn smiles into sneers and peace into war. And I wonder about the maturity of our people, my nation, in the face of future crises that will inevitably arise.

I have my own sense of right and wrong. I detest and am in sorrow over the spectacle of people killing people, of the rich allowing the poor to starve, of people being denied their right to speak freely, of nations not being allowed to choose freely their own rulers, of governments lying to those they govern. These values are not shared widely, even in our own nation. Last night Henry Kissinger delivered an elegant, thoughtful and balanced speech. In it he made a plea for consensus. I've heard that song already. Power seeks consensus. If you can convince people that you're right, you don't have to force them to follow you. Consensus has a way of locking everyone in, intellectually and politically. It has a way of generating paranoia, as the desire for consensus is transformed into the demand for unanimity. Dissent becomes difficult if not impossible.

Stanley Hoffmann talked about co-option. We've seen that too. How easy it is to take an idea offered in good faith from outside the government as an alternative to policy. To stick it in your speech and therefore smash critics. I don't think the alternative to consensus is chaos. I think we can manage by arguing with each other, as long as there is some tolerance. I am concerned not only for the constitutional right of dissent in our country nowadays, but for the political feasibility of dissent, when consensus consumes us all. What I hope for is not a new consensus in the national interest of the United States but a new acceptance of dissent.

Leslie Gelb is National Security Correspondent, Washington Bureau, **The New York Times.**

Frances FitzGerald:

I find it a puzzling task to speak on the subject of the
national interest of the United States. My experience as a
journalist has thus far been with people who are more or
less the victims of American policy, the Cubans and the
Vietnamese. And what has impressed me is their point of
view. It seems to me that while we discuss the issue of
our foreign policy, we ought to bear in mind that the
greatest problem for many people in this world is dealing
with us, and not in the abstract, either. They deal with us
day by day, through our AID programs, our corporations,
and our B-52s. Stanley Hoffmann has spoken about the
need for community rather than a simple grouping of
forces. It seems to me we are now very far from that.
Mr. Hutchins quoted Lincoln on his desire to be neither a
master nor a slave. But that is, in so many cases, exactly
the relationship that the United States has created
elsewhere in the world. Foreign policy is unfortunately
not, as Secretary Kissinger said, simply the relationship
between sovereign states. The formal trappings of
sovereignty, of membership in the United Nations,
belong to almost everyone these days. But the real
international situation remains in so many cases that of
metropolis and colony, of tyrant and victim. Or a
non-relationship, a difference in life styles so great that
Americans appear to other people like people of a
different race or like Martians.

I find myself in substantial agreement with Messrs.
Hoffmann, Barnet and Tucker, but I also find it very hard
to speak in abstractions. And, like Mr. Gelb, I find it
difficult to continue a discussion on foreign policy always
in a spirit of sweet reason. Why? Because the Indochina
war is not yet over. After thirteen years and three or
perhaps four million Indochinese dead, we are still
supporting, maintaining and supplying that destruction.
The so-called peace agreements signed in January took
American soldiers out of the battles, but it changed

nothing for the Indochinese. Is that what Secretary Kissinger means when he speaks of a compromise? It's hard to be reasonable in face of such supreme reason. And it's hard to stay reasonable in the face of recent events in Chile. The United States, through its subsidiaries, international banks and large corporations, deliberately destroyed the economy of a dependent country. Our aid went only to the armed forces, making a military *coup* against a democratically-elected government close to inevitable.

This is not the first of such interventions; it is only the most recent. Right now it is difficult to find a country in the so-called third world where the U.S. has heavy investment that does not have a military government or a dictatorial régime. Dictatorships, corruption, elitism, and so forth are not the result of some mystical nature of Asians or Latin Americans. The régimes of South Korea, Brazil, the Philippines and Greece, have been created by the United States. They are the product of the deformation we have made in their domestic structures of power. And it is considered perfectly just for Americans to protect these governments. Furthermore as we support these governments, we are holding a pistol to the head of communist régimes. War, as Solzhenitsyn reminds us, is not the only form of violence. Since World War II the United States has wreaked unparalleled violence on the small countries of the world. In most cases we have bent these small powers to our will. Vietnam was the exception, the exception because of the enormous and perhaps unfathomable resistance of the Vietnamese. We cannot assume that this violence and this bullying will stop with what may be a détente between the great powers. On the contrary, the détente may serve only to give more latitude to such bullying, both by the United States and by the Soviet Union. Détente may mean simply a license for the great to tyrannize the small. Is such tyranny in the interest of the United States? I hope not. I think not. But I do know that the rhetoric, some of which we heard from Mr. Kissinger about the American role in the defense of freedom and morality is just that, rhetoric. As yet there is no real sense of community, and that's what we need.

Frances FitzGerald is the author of Fire in the Lake, *a study of the war in Vietnam.*

Hoffmann:

The more I listen to the discussion the more I sympathize with my old friend Leslie Gelb. There's a great virtue in being an agnostic. It would be very difficult to reconcile all of the truths that we have heard here. So I'd like to make a few scattered and staccato remarks on some of the points that have been made. I agree with Hans Morgenthau that there is in the balance of power something close to the law of gravity. But he, himself, when he pointed out how obsolete many of our conceptions are, made the point that by contrast with the maintenance of military equilibrium between the main competitors the notion of a balance-of-power *system*, which has its own set of rules (which he himself in his books defines most eloquently), is by now obsolete. That any new kind of system will have to be based on a certain form of military equilibrium is, of course, true. But that the rules of the game will have to be different from the rules of the balance-of-power systems of the past, I think he would be the first to admit.

It is precisely because the world we're moving into is so radically different that the debate between those who argue about the divisibility of peace, and those who cling to the notion of its indivisibility, is somewhat artificial. I agree with Mr. Tucker that in a nuclear world the divisibility of peace is a far greater reality than before. I think one should not confuse two very different notions here. One is that in a nuclear world there is indeed a chance of limiting the use of force regionally, of preventing the use of force from escalating all over the planet when a conflict breaks out in a certain area. I think we are witnessing this right now. But this does not mean that peace is indeed divisible in one quite different sense.

Trouble is not divisible. Even if military trouble may be contained in a given area, what is likely to happen is the spread, the contagion of trouble to other areas of international politics. To cite one by its very short name: oil. And in this sense there is no divisibility of peace. There are spreading waves from a limited military conflict to the other chessboards of international politics, and this is precisely why some measure of community is needed. But this is not easy as shown by the remarks of Frances FitzGerald.

Implied both in Frances FitzGerald's remarks and in some of Mr. Barnet's was the notion that somehow everything that happens in the world which is evil is very largely the fault of the United States. Now it seems to me that in regard to Vietnam a very good case can indeed be made for this. But I am not sure that if the United States somehow removed itself from the world and went after its own business in the fashion that Mr. Barnet suggests there would not still be an enormous amount of evil and brutalization. One of the tragedies is that in many parts of the world, and not only the developing areas, the choice is a choice of *who* will brutalize the population. To be sure, there is much to be said for a policy which will proclaim at least that the United States will stop brutalizing others, either from the outside or from the inside. But it would not be an answer to the problem, and we would still have to face the problem of what happens if the brutalization is done by our own main rivals, or is done in a way which does indeed harm either American interests or American ideals.

This brings me to the main point which has been clearly at the heart of this discussion. We have heard quite eloquently stated an argument, with which I entirely agree, about the need to disentangle American foreign policy from private American interests, notably the interests of American corporations abroad. I say American because the word multinational is a marvelous facade for American corporations. But we have heard equally eloquent pleas for reinvigorating the American ethos, and for having official policy be, so to speak, the carrier of that ethos. Unfortunately, for many Americans the worldwide spread of free enterprise is part of the American ethos. How do you disentangle all of this? Well, you can say that the ideal foreign policy should be disentangled completely from everything which is not in the cold, calculated national interest. That would leave out all private interests or private ideals. The problem, however, is that this is not very easy in a democracy at present. We have the extraordinary paradox of a nation in which state and society are really quite separate, but in which many of its representatives insist on voting for an amendment that would, in effect, require the state to change somebody else's society. That effort is aimed at a totalitarian régime in which the state completely controls the society, and lectures us daily about the need to separate foreign policy from intervention in domestic affairs! This simply shows that this very old-fashioned distinction is indeed not tenable. But if it is no longer tenable, especially in a democracy, how do you disentangle that part of the national ethos which you find good, and which you would like to spread, from the part which you find repulsive? What may be repulsive to some of us may be the best part of the national ethos to others. Is forcing others to be humane in our sense any more legitimate than forcing others to accept our kind of economic system because we consider it to be more rational or effective? I raise the question, and I think the only way of answering it is to try to find if there is sufficient agreement to define what an ideal world community would be. But I do not think we would get this kind of agreement very easily. I, too, am somewhat afraid of the paranoia which consensus often creates. Unless one has what might be called a "uniting threat," I think both we, as outside critics, and the officials who try to shape policy, are tangled in a web of difficulties and contradictions for which one can ask, to use one of Secretary Kissinger's favorite words, "compassion." But it would be absolutely pretentious for us to say that we have an answer to it.

Will:

There is nothing quite as traditional through the ages as scholars disparaging, as Mr. Hoffmann does, the wisdom of the ages and the constructs of scholars. But changes in the basic facts of political life, facts about life within political communities, or about relations between communities, are rarely as rapid and shattering as predicted by scholars whose profession it is to divine the direction and shape of change.

Of course, today, as usual, there are real and significant changes taking place. Mr. Hoffmann is right to emphasize the challenge to nations by transnational forces, especially economic forces. But it still seems reasonable to assume that, to the extent these forces are tamed, they will be tamed by nations for national purposes. I only wish Mr. Hoffmann had included in his analysis some appraisal of volatile transnational moral forces of the sort loosed by Soviet Jews and dissidents. These moral forces have a way of getting mixed up in transnational economic forces; they also demand national responses from various nations because nations, unlike the international community, are not fictions. Mr. Hoffmann is rightly concerned by internal U.S. opposition to the kind of transformation he approves in the U.S. world role. He expects opposition from, among others, and I quote, "All those in the bureaucracy and the economy who have acquired a stake in the preservation of the U.S. world system." Now, if we accept Mr. Hoffmann's highly-charged label for the current situation in the U.S. world system, if in this situation the U.S. economy is as dependent as Mr. Hoffmann says it is on that U.S. world system, then isn't it likely that those who will oppose a substantial alteration of the current U.S. role in the world will include most of those interested in the continuing functioning of the U.S. economy, which is to say, most Americans?

Mr. Hoffman warns that if the kind of transformation he favors comes to pass, "We will have to see ourselves again as one player among many, rather than as a specially-anointed missionary or teacher." Such distinctions between being one player among many and being an anointed missionary have an artificial clarity that distorts the past and muddies the future. The U.S. should want to be, and probably cannot help but be, the most important player in world politics. But this does not mean our importance must be missionary. Mr. Hoffmann says that increasingly world politics cannot be defined only as a contest of states. That is true. But it is also true that, to the extent that world politics is not a contest of states, it is hard to identify the players. I accept for the United States that which most American presidents since Lincoln and every president since Franklin Roosevelt have accepted—the distinction that former Ambassador to the U.S.S.R. "Chip" Bohlen makes with regard to the Soviet Union—the distinction between the U.S. as a country and the U.S. as a cause. Because we cannot help but be powerful we cannot be indifferent to the potential for using our power, peacefully, to promote humane values beyond our borders. We can choose to use our power or not to use it, but we must choose. It is not helpful to imply that any decision to use national power on behalf of humane values is a missionary caper. Between missionary zealotry and a dogmatic refusal to use available power for moral purposes lies a middle ground where prudent, moderate men can work to improve the world without endangering it.

Norton Ginsburg:

Perhaps I can add something of my own as we begin to move toward the end of the session. I'm struck by the degree of consensus among all the principals concerning the near identity, indeed the intimacy, between foreign and domestic policy. There is some difference of view as to what extent this is a new situation, and Professor Morgenthau has suggested it in fact is not; but I don't think it's a conventional view or one that is as widely held, perhaps, as it seems to be among the experts at this table.

I'm also struck with at least a partial consensus among the speakers about the need for developing those kinds of policies relating to other countries, which recognize the changing rank-ordering of basic power—economic power—among the countries of the world, which recognize that, in effect, the United States may no longer properly be regarded as *the* primate state and therefore must play a more modest role in world affairs. At the same time, however, circumstances require recognition of the fact that the United States, by virtue of its enormous resource endowment, population, and technology, continues and will continue to be enormously powerful, and by its very existence thus will have an important impact on other countries that may or may not be a consequence of deliberate American policies. This is not the same as urging simply that we substitute the word "multinodality" in place of the word "bipolarity," for it seems to me that they are qualitatively different.

The third point that impressed me is recognition of the need for developing and maintaining relations which can serve as bridges between the rich and the poor countries. There is nothing new about this, of course, but to the extent that this problem has been part of our foreign policy processes at all, we have dealt with it very poorly. As is well known, the gap between the rich and the poor in this world is increasing steadily. Moreover, one world scenario would suggest that the richer countries will detach themselves increasingly from the poorer ones because, by one of the great ironies of historical geography, the richer countries are far better endowed with what they need, except perhaps for petroleum, than the poorer countries, and they also have the technology to get much more of what they need from the oceans and the ocean bed, for example, than the poorer countries. It follows then that poverty in the world, of course, is not created by the United States, even though we may have contributed to it in some places. Modernization, too, whatever that means, is not our creation, but we have been and still are a model that other people, almost without deliberation, seem to want to emulate, even though that model, we all agree, may not be the most admirable.

This, then, leads to the point that Professor Hoffmann underscored: the need for international, transnational, global institutions to manage and order relationships that are no longer amenable to strictly conventional international types of arrangements. I don't mean to suggest that the United Nations is perhaps not the best device now available by which to develop such institutional arrangements. Certainly Senator Fulbright was eloquent about that point yesterday. But we need to lend our thoughts—and we have been doing this at the Center I might add—to the need for new kinds of global institutions that will work in ways that the United Nations cannot. We don't know what they will be. On the other hand, it's perfectly clear that although the idea of "one world" is an old one that extends from Mackinder to Wendell Wilkie, the recognition of it as a fact widely held is something that is different today from the pre-World War II period. This recognition has come upon us gradually, but there isn't any doubt that almost all thoughtful people hold to it, whereas in the 1930s, for example, they did not.

Finally, I'm impressed by the need for, if you like, redefinitions or, better, for clarification and understanding, particularly for laymen like myself and many of the people in this audience, of what old terms still in use have come to mean as the contexts for them have been transformed. The "balance of power" phrase to which reference has been made by several speakers is a good example. What we learned it meant when I was a college student is really very different today, even though the term is in current use and has continued validity.

Norton Ginsburg is Dean of the Center for the Study of Democratic Institutions.

Herschelle Challenor:

I think I would make a stronger case than Marshall Shulman made about United States-Soviet tensions. He contends that tensions are now maintained at lower levels. And I think there is some historical evidence that indeed the Soviets and the Americans have a sort of hands-off policy with respect to any involvement in each other's sphere of influence. In 1960, as you know, the Soviets backed down on their effort to give unilateral military assistance to what was then the Congo during the Congo crisis. In 1961, of course, we had the Berlin Wall crisis, meaning that the United States spoke much but did little. In 1963, the Cuban missile crisis. Later in the 1960s, Czechoslovakia, where the United States took no concrete action. In 1972, the mining of Haiphong did nothing to prevent the Moscow summit meeting. So I think there's evidence that both sides have not been willing to risk nuclear confrontation with the other in order to make gains in other areas of the world.

Then there is the point Mr. Shulman raises about the importance of domestic pressure. He's speaking specifically to the question of the exit tax for Soviet Jews. Yet a stronger case can be made for some attempt to modify the domestic policies of South Africa. The United Nations has already declared that apartheid in South Africa is a threat to the peace and international security and therefore is not contained within Article 2, Section 4, which prevents member states from getting involved in domestic conflicts of other member states. We're dealing with a minority that tries to suppress, and very effectively suppresses, a majority. And yet there is no hue and cry in this country about this kind of injustice. Moreover, it is important to note that avoiding nuclear war with a superpower is at stake in the Soviet-American case, while there is no persuasive economic or military reason for the United States to court South Africa.

Herschelle Challenor, an American Political Science Association Congressional Fellow, is Professor of Political Science at Brooklyn College, City University of New York.

Morton Halperin:

It would be a mistake if we proceeded in this conference with a will to forget what the United States has been doing in the world over the past several years. The rest of the people in the world have certainly not forgotten. I believe it was Florence Nightingale who said that the first obligation of hospitals was not to spread disease. This is an important analogy for us to bear in mind when we hear the injunction that the United States should go out and do good in the world. It is hard for me to believe that those who have been the particular focus of our attention in the world over the past decade feel that they're better off as a result of our interventions, or that the American claim to a moral leadership in the world can any longer be taken seriously. For the people of Indochina, clearly, this is at best a bitter joke and a horrible reality. The Koreans have learned again recently that their close association with the United States is no guarantee of the spread of democracy or of freedom. It is difficult for me to believe that the people of Greece or the people of Chile are better off in any way that conforms to our ideals because of their association with us. The Secretary of State has just assured us that the United States always stands on the side of freedom and always presses for freedom. I suspect that this is an analysis of the world for which he would not get a very good grade if he took an examination in any of these countries.

As human beings we can care, and must care, about what happens to other human beings throughout the world. But as realistic observers of world affairs, and as realistic citizens of the United States, I think we have to ask ourselves: What have we learned from the past about how the American government will behave when we send it out into the world in our name? We have to ask ourselves whether the urging of a more active American role will in fact bring the kind of benevolent result that we would like, or whether it will bring the kind of result that it has brought in the past.

It seems to me that from that perspective we can do best to urge that our government do less, that it focus on what has to be done at home, that it recognize that peace is indeed divisible and that the problems of the world cannot be solved by us, and that when we try we are as likely to exacerbate them as to ease them. We must, therefore, concentrate, when we deal with the world, on our real interest, on what really is at stake in terms of our own security, in terms of protecting our own institutions and our own way of life.

Morton Halperin is a Senior Fellow at The Brookings Institution and former Deputy Assistant Secretary of Defense.

David Horowitz:

One would have thought that a conference on the national interests of the United States, convened at this moment in the nation's history by such a body as the Center for the Study of Democratic Institutions, would have been the occasion for profound national soul-searching, a fundamental reappraisal of the assumptions on which the national policy and enterprise are based. We are now disengaged from the most criminal war in our history, a war against a technologically defenseless people which ranks with the worst atrocities ever committed by one portion of the human race against another. We have only recently witnessed our government move dramatically toward a détente with China and the Soviet Union, thereby exposing the Cold War myth of aggressive communist expansionism and necessary American containment, in whose name we have killed more than four million people in the underdeveloped world, squandered more than a trillion dollars of socially-needed resources and bankrupted the nation morally, politically and economically over the last quarter of a century. In these circumstances one would have thought that this convocation would have taken a long hard look at the realities of American foreign policy, at the definition of the national interest that has carried such a curse of misery and destruction to the postwar world. And a long, hard look at the governing principles which have bequeathed to us such a legacy of political corruption and moral disintegration here at home. One would have thought that such a gathering would have been prepared to ask itself the hard question, whether this curse does not lie in the deep structures of national experience and not just in the momentary policies of the postwar administrations, the rise of the military-industrial complex, or the anti-communist phobia that pervaded the national consciousness in the Cold War years. The question is whether its roots do not lie in the very character of the American enterprise and ambition, whether Vietnam is not so much a betrayal of the American tradition as its fulfillment. But these are not at all the questions the participants in this convocation have come to discuss. Instead, they appear to regard themselves as a self-appointed advisory group to the present Administration, to point out opportunities which Washington might not otherwise perceive for the prosecution of the national interest as it is presently and officially conceived. The appearance of Secretary of State Kissinger as a guest of honor at this affair seems to symbolize that fact—as though there is a consensus concerning the basic conception of the national interest that binds Mr. Kissinger and the rest of us, those here and those mostly unrepresented on these panels: black people, Chicanos, the working class and the poor. The ghosts of this conference are those whose privilege as Americans begins and ends with the right to die in democracy's wars. For my own part, I think that Mr. Kissinger's presence symbolizes something else. It symbolizes how deep and corrupting the lust for power is in our society even among men of good will. It symbolizes the sickness that pervades the body politic at this stage in the nation's decline when the state has become such an absolute that men will cling to it even though it betrays everything that they hold dear. The government that Secretary Kissinger represents is a gangster régime. It is not legitimate even by the limited precepts of the democratic system as we know it; it has committed murder on a colossal scale internationally, while domestically it has usurped power by fraud and deception. These are the men who lied to us to create the Cold War, lied to us to lead us into Indochina, and will go on lying to us because they represent a system in which virtue is identified with their own privilege and power. Unfortunately, however, although they have betrayed both the high ideals of American democracy and the specific injunctions of the U.S. Constitution, Nixon and Kissinger have not strayed far from the traditional paths of American power. The murder of Vietnam is but the most recent massacre on that frontier of freedom which has been expanding since the Mayflower landed, and has dashed its prophets' hopes against the shores of its triumphs, leaving the dead of vanquished nations strewn as monuments in its wake.

Our philosophical need as a nation, we are told, is to change our vision of the world and of our place in it so that we can extend the moral basis on which this country was founded and has grown, extend it not only to include all Americans but also people elsewhere whose physical and spiritual futures are bound up with our own. How is this a change in America's vision of itself as the last best hope of mankind, that fraudulent dream in whose name all its crimes have been committed? We took a continent by chicanery and conquest; we built a society on slavery and servitude, and we proclaimed to the world that this was freedom and we were its prophets. It is precisely the combination of limitless moral arrogance and ruthless practical self-aggrandizement that constitutes the true moral basis on which our nation was founded and under which it has grown so great. And it is the refusal to recognize this, to confront the legacy and its responsibilities, which is the root cause of our present predicament. Why are we in Vietnam? Because, as President Kennedy told us, invoking the words of Tom Paine, our cause is the cause of all mankind. Because, as President Johnson told us, we are responsible for the maintenance of freedom around the world. For moral guidance we are offered the same national self-deception which has always inspired America's course of conquest in the past. Nor does intellect, as it is represented here by Mr. Shulman, have anything more useful to offer. We are told by him that our main long-term objective as a nation must be to draw our adversaries into constructive participation in the international system and that the international system is to be understood as a codification of civilized practices among nations, not for the purpose of preserving the *status quo* but for the purpose of assuring that the process of change among nations can be as orderly as possible with a minimum of violence and a maximum of respect for the wishes of the people involved. The paramount purpose of our foreign policy, then, would be to encourage our adversaries who do not share this view of civilized international order to see their own self-interests and security in this kind of international environment.

The mind boggles at the intellectual and moral arrogance of such a formulation. This is the same smug line served up by U.S. Secretaries of State from Jimmy Byrnes and Dean Acheson to Dean Rusk and Henry Kissinger. It forgets that we are the international outlaws, the violators of international order and the purveyors of international violence who have to learn to respect civilized codes of behavior. We are the wreckers of international agreements, the compulsive interveners in the affairs of other nations and the global guardians of oppressive social and economic *status quo*. Our intellectual and moral sense is blind to the realities of our international course. We are not at the end, however, but rather on the threshold of America's agony in the world. The new balance of power is more unstable and potentially far more dangerous than the old. As for America itself, not until the imperial vision is abandoned, not until the corporate foundations of the empire are dissolved, not until the military arm is withdrawn from Asia, from Latin America, from Europe and Africa will the United States begin to be a positive force in the international system. And not until then will its true national interest begin to be served.

We have men on these panels who have been deeply involved in all the duplicities of the last years, intimately involved in using very noble American ideals and very goodhearted American people to wage atrocities throughout the world. While having some of them on the panels would have created a kind of dialogue and conflict which could have illuminated these kinds of questions, the way they are stacked and the way this whole convocation is stacked makes it impossible for anybody to see the light through all the darkness. I hope the next time there is a *Pacem in Terris* the panels will be very different.

David Horowitz is an editorial writer for Ramparts *magazine.*

Ronald Steel:

I don't deplore the enthusiasm shown by the audience for Mr. Horowitz's presentation, and I share much of his indignation. I do feel it is very necessary. But perhaps we also have to move on to something beyond condemning ourselves as the scourge of the earth and the most evil nation to walk the planet and examine what it is we can do now. Perhaps atonement might be the word to describe what our policy should be in the post-Vietnam era. But simply to go through the world today with a sense of profound guilt, of worthlessness and moral depravity, I think is not a very useful point of departure for our foreign policy.

I deplore the attitude of American exceptionalism, that sees this country as the salvation of the world. But the opposite side of that coin, to see America as responsible for every evil that happens everywhere, is perhaps an equal form of arrogance. The kind of debate over national interest taking place here today is very strange for many of us. There is a whole new dimension emerging from the old labels to which we've become so accustomed, but which now seem so obsolete. As Yeats said, the center doesn't hold. The traditional Left, the people who had been the most assertive critics of American foreign policy, are now speaking in a language that we've come to associate with the defenders of Cold War policy. They speak in terms of national interest and security.

I thought it was instructive this morning that the person who was most concerned with moral values in American foreign policy was the Washington editor of the *National Review.* In many cases the Right and Left seem to be changing places. No one knows what is Right and what is Left any more in this debate. There's been a profound transformation in the style of American foreign policy, in the vocabulary of American foreign policy. The question is whether that transformation is also one of substance. We have been reminded that the President has stated that our world will presumably be a safer one if all the nations are in balance. But this vision of a pentagonal juggling act sounds suspiciously like the kind of nine-teenth century diplomacy which Wilson inveighed against and Cordell Hull promised was to be forever eliminated. There was a reason for that, because statesmen believed that power-balancing led to two cataclysmic wars within a generation. But now, like so many of yesterday's styles, the old formula has been exhumed and dusted off and given a patina of responsibility and billed as the last word in up-to-date diplomacy.

One might be tempted to say with the ancients that there is indeed nothing new under the sun. But the style is different. We perhaps have not yet returned to that case described by the English statesman, Canning, where every nation was for itself and God for us all. But with the breakup of the Cold War alliances and the increas-ingly vicious trade competition between the industrialized nations, we may be coming to that. Today American foreign policy-makers, for the first time since they began to feel a mortal longing stirring in them a quarter century ago when the sun ceased to set on our empire, are beginning to feel a cold draft. So many of the assump-tions that we took for granted now have to be demon-strated. And quite often those assumptions turn out to be false. We see the old dictum of Palmerston being brushed off and quoted approvingly whenever our trade balance gets unduly out of line. Palmerston said, "We have permanent adversaries and no permanent allies; our interests alone are eternal."

But what are our interests? Today we are less sure of them than we have ever been. Once we thought it was isolation, then we thought it was universal responsibility for the fate of mankind. Now some of us think it's universal guilt for the state of mankind. But we aren't sure what it is. There's such a fear of rocking the boat, a fear that change in itself, unless it's terribly gradual, might be a bad thing; that foreign policy preoccupation in many cases has been reduced to making sure we have enough oil to keep warm this winter. We may now be reaching a state where we have neither permanent allies nor permanent adversaries, but we certainly continue to have permanent entanglements. And entanglements is perhaps the most charitable word we can use to describe our relations with a good many nations within our camp. Precisely how to define that camp is a problem of no mean dimensions. During the heyday of the Cold War it was easy enough. Whatever wasn't in their camp was in ours, except for a few of the moral neutrals. But anti-communism at that time became synonymous with the Free World, that catch-all phrase, which was very useful as long as it wasn't examined closely. But we don't even know what our camp is now. We don't know who our allies are, who our enemies are.

At a time when we are assiduously wooing both Peking and Moscow, it is very difficult to claim that we are trying to rally our friends around the banner of anti-communism. And considering some of the régimes which we support, and which look to us for sustenance, the term Free World is about as descriptive as the term Holy Roman Empire, and that, as we know, was neither holy nor Roman nor an empire. Not only do we no longer know who our friends are, but we don't know who our adversaries are supposed to be. Is our enemy Soviet Russia, which we beseech to buy our grain and which tries to lure us into an alliance against China? Or is it the governing régime of a country like South Vietnam, which has demanded and received our lives, our fortunes and our sacred honor? As Marshall Shulman has shown, we are engaged in both competition and cooperation with our Cold War adversaries. Yet the same words could well be used to describe our relations with our erstwhile allies. It may be that the world is not necessarily getting more complex, but that our perceptions are catching up with realities. In this real world our relations with our adversaries are crucial.

I agree with Mr. Shulman that we should try to stabilize the military competition and strengthen restraints against great power exploitation of local conflict situations. I certainly cannot disagree with appeals for equitable economic relations among the rich and poor nations, as well as for the moral concern that transcends economic and political competition. Translating that into action, I think, is going to be much more difficult, precisely because that moral concern does not at the moment exist. It should exist; perhaps it will exist, and it should be our objective to bring it to the forefront of our foreign policy-makers.

Perhaps this is the argument around which the whole discussion of the Jackson amendment revolves. It's been very instructive to me to see the way in which, and the reasons for which people are lined up on one side of this argument or the other. As Morton Halperin says, perhaps we're choosing sides here. My side, I find surprisingly enough, is with Senator Jackson. A moral foreign policy means accommodations with our adversaries that do not betray our own values. It means recognition that there are values which transcend expediency, power politics, and changing definitions of the national interest. We have heard the Secretary of State make what seemed to me a quite remarkable statement when he said that "a nation's values determine what is just." I found that rather outrageous. What if the nation's values involve repression or injustice or even genocide?

We certainly have had enough of moralizing in foreign policy. We've had enough self-justification in foreign policy. But in moving toward a new realism we should remember that justice is a reality that lies outside of transcending temporary values and not merely a euphemism for whatever today's definition of national interest might be. There is no inherent contradiction between a moral foreign policy and an enlightened conception of the national interest. In our hot pursuit of the latter, there is a real danger of betraying the former.

Ronald Steel is a Visting Lecturer at Yale University and a former U.S. Foreign Service officer.

REFERENCE MATTER

Appendix

PACEM IN TERRIS I
New York City, February 17-20, 1965

Ten years ago the encyclical of Pope John XXIII, *Pacem in Terris*, entered history—in the words of French Monsignor Bernard Lalande—like *"un coup de tonnerre."* Robert M. Hutchins recognized it as "one of the most profound and significant documents of our age," and put the Center's Fellows to work analyzing its implications for a major turn-around in world affairs. Of it, Hutchins said: "It was no accident that John XXIII had emphasized, as did Thomas Aquinas before him, that peace is the work of charity and justice, that peace is not merely the absence of war, that peace is the nature of human life everywhere. *Pacem in Terris* began appropriately with a list of human rights. The Pope said: 'The fundamental principle upon which our present peace depends must be replaced by another.' Thus he consigned nuclear arms, nationalism, colonialism, racism, and non-constitutional regimes to the wastebasket of history. He rejected the devil theory of politics, asserting that 'the same moral law which governs relations between individual human beings serves also to regulate the relations of political communities with each other.'"

Two years later the reverberation from the great moral thunderclap that had sounded from Rome seemed to be dying away. So it was that the Center convened in New York, February 1965, *Pacem in Terris I,* an international convocation dedicated to the proposition that the encyclical John XXIII addressed to all men and all nations should not be forgotten. Its recommendations provided the agenda for a great gathering of world secular and spiritual leaders.

The convocation opened with a plenary session in the hall of the General Assembly at the United Nations. It brought together statesmen, scholars, and other "movers and shakers" from socialist and non-socialist states, among then the Secretary-General of the United Nations; the president of the U.N. General Assembly and two of its former presidents; the Vice President and Chief Justice of the United States, an Associate Justice and four U.S. senators; the Belgian Prime Minister Paul-Henri Spaak; the Italian Deputy Prime Minister, Pietro Nenni; leading public figures from the U.S.S.R., Poland and Yugoslavia; two Justices of the World Court; historian Arnold Toynbee, and theologian Paul Tillich.

Robert M. Hutchins, at the Convocation's outset, told the twenty-five hundred participants: "This is not an ecumenical council assembled to debate religious topics. This is a political meeting. The question is: How can we make peace, not peace through the dreadful mechanisms of terror, but peace, pure, simple and durable? If the principles of *Pacem in Terris* are sound, how can they be carried out in the world as it is? If they are unsound, what principles are sound?"

Secretary-General U Thant observed: "Pope John was no intruder in the dust of the political arena. He knew that hard lines could no longer be drawn between what was happening to the human estate, and what was happening to the human soul . . . . It is not for me, a Buddhist, to speculate on his religious significance, but I believe that later historians will regard him as one of the principal spokesmen and architects for vital change in the twentieth century . . . . Pope John recognized that the age of hiding places had come to an end. For the first time, everyone inside the world enclosure was potentially vulnerable to the failure of even well-intentioned men to move beyond old and inadequate responses and methods."

The then Vice President, Hubert Humphrey, said, "*Pacem in Terris* offers a public philosophy for a nuclear era." The Pope had not written "a Utopian blueprint for world peace, presupposing a sudden change in the nature of man. Rather the encyclical presented a call to action to leaders of nations, presupposing only a gradual change in human institutions . . . the building of a world community."

Norman Cousins, who had served in a private capacity as emissary between Pope John, President John F. Kennedy and Chairman Nikita Khrushchev during the post Cuban missile crisis period, said that "space flights, nuclear energy and all other of modern man's spectacular achievements did not have the impress on history of an eighty-one year-old man dying of cancer, using the Papacy to make not just his own Church but all churches fully relevant and fully alive in the cause of human unity and peace. . . . Human advocacy harnessed to powerful ideas continues to be the prime mover. The peace sought by Pope John need not be unattainable once belief in ideas is put ahead of belief in moving parts."

A great theologian raised the question of whether human nature is capable of creating peace on earth. Paul Tillich observed that man's will being hopelessly ambiguous, one should not address an encyclical to "all men of good will: but to all men, since there is bad in the best and good in the worst." Tillich drew a distinction between hope for a world ruled by peace, justice and love, and hope for a world community capable of avoiding self-destruction. He named several grounds for this kind of hope, including the "community of fear" created by the prospect of nuclear war. This ground, he said, at least makes the conflicting powers conscious that there is such a thing as "mankind with a common destiny."

Psychiatrist Jerome Frank pointed out that while man is both killer and saint, modern war is an elaborate social institution that has to be taught to each generation and can be untaught as well. The problem, thought Frank, is not how to create total peace on earth, but how to make the world safe from man's natural aggressiveness by limiting the scope of his conflicts.

The problem of this duality in man's nature and the avoidance of conflict could best be answered, said Grenville Clark, author of *World Peace Through World Law,* by the limiting of national sovereignty. Nations must assign powers to a world body sufficient to enact and enforce laws binding on all nations. "Such powers," Clark stressed, "can only be described as those of government, i.e., a world government." The need for new forms of world governance, in light of the increasing obsolescence of national sovereignty, was a recurrent theme from the Convocation's beginning to its end.

Ambassador Luis Quintanilla, of Mexico, favored revising the United Nations Charter, enlarging the Security Council, abolishing the veto, weighting Assembly votes to represent populations, and giving the organization a monopoly of nuclear force. The chairman of the Constitution Revision Commission of Japan, Kenzo Takayanagi, reported that his Commission had decided *not* to recommend any change in Japan's famous "pacifist" clause, Article IX of the Constitution, which renounces Japan's sovereign right to wage war and possess armaments.

These views met counterargument from believers in "piecemeal" peacekeeping. World Court Judge Muhammad Zafrulla Khan, of Pakistan, pointed out that only a fully sovereign nation can make a firm treaty, or even cede part of its sovereignty to the authority of world law. His U.S. colleague on the World Court, Philip Jessup, emphasized the coral-like way in which law grows; the fact that much international behavior, such as air routes, mail and weather information is already governed by a network of law, which can and does grow; and that "leg over leg the dog went to Dover."

The Convocation turned to discussion of what was then only barely mentionable: "peaceful coexistence." William Fulbright, chairman of the Senate Foreign Relations Committee, said that national ideology, or a coherent system of values, is a source of great strength and creative energy, but also of "appalling danger," since it tends to impose on others "the tyranny of abstract ideas." He proposed that both the United States and the Soviet Union, in order to make peaceful coexistence less precarious, should subordinate their respective ideologies to "the human requirements of a changing world." The Russians, Yevgenyi Zhukov and N.N. Inozemtsev, both leading Party theoreticians, agreed in part with Fulbright.

The Russians declared that states with different social systems can and must coexist, but only on the basis of sovereign equality and noninterference; there can be no coexistence between "oppressor and oppressed." Inozemtsev said Marxist-Leninist ideology does not advocate the export of revolutions and opposes "the export of counter-revolutions."

"Wars of liberation," Zhukov said, "are legitimate exceptions to the Soviet opposition to war." The "coexistence" discussants found it difficult to agree on anything except Fulbright's plea for mutual tolerance and "the cultivation of a spirit in which nations are more interested in solving problems than in proving theories."

Former Ambassador to the U.S.S.R. and Yugoslavia, George F. Kennan, called for sweeping changes in our European policy, to the point of military disengagement in Germany, and a revision of U.S. assumptions—which provided the *raison d'être* for NATO—about Soviet aggressive intentions.

Abba Eban of Israel declared that after millennia of "national histories, mankind has entered the first era of global history." He proposed that all heads of state devote one week of their working year exclusively to the problems of "the human nation." He set forth an agenda: overpopulation, malnutrition, illiteracy, gross inequality of incomes, and the repair of the physical damage man has done to his planet.

The response to Eban's speech demonstrated that the ecumenical spirit invoked by John XXIII was still alive. It could be said to have been translated into political reality by a Convocation at which, for the first time, leaders of the European Communist bloc mingled openly with their counterparts from the West in informal circumstances where no one was an official delegate bound by his nation's formal view—and where the effort was not aimed at national advantage, or even ultimate agreement, but at greater common understanding.

But even as the delegates gathered in New York, the war in Southeast Asia was escalating, and with it the Cold War tensions between East and West.

PACEM IN TERRIS II
Geneva, Switzerland, May 28-31, 1967

Pacem in Terris I ended with a call from those present for a continuation of the effort. In response, the Center a year later assembled at the Palais des Nations in Geneva advisers from the United Nations, the United States, the Soviet Union, Great Britain, Japan, the United Arab Republic, Poland, France, Cambodia and Mexico to consider the possibilities of another convocation in the light of deteriorating international relations. To them Robert M. Hutchins addressed two primary questions: Could the People's Republic of China be persuaded to attend *Pacem in Terris II*? If not, was there any point in discussing the problems of world order with a fourth of the world's people unrepresented? There was scant optimism about the first, but positive response to the second. Academician N.N. Inozemtsev of the U.S.S.R., observing that in any case the Vietnam conflict would be bound to dominate the next *Pacem in Terris* Convocation, suggested a concentrated effort to bring in Hanoi and thereby initiate a direct American contact that might open the way for peace in Southeast Asia.

The Frenchmen present, Pierre Mendès-France, Premier of France at the time of the defeat at Dien Bien Phu, Ambassador Jean Chauvel, a China expert who had recently returned from Peking via Hanoi, and Xavier Deniau, ranking Gaullist member of the Foreign Affairs Committee of the National Assembly, agreed to arrange with the North Vietnamese representative in Paris to transmit to Hanoi a letter suggesting a meeting with representatives of the Center.

In the meantime, another Center adviser, Ambassador Luis Quintanilla of Mexico, departed for Peking to extend the Center's invitation to participate in *Pacem in Terris II*. After receiving a polite rebuff, he proceeded to Hanoi for a private audience with Ho Chi Minh, who indicated he would receive representatives from the Center to discuss Hanoi's participation. Harry Ashmore, Center president, and the late William Baggs, editor of the Miami *News* and a Center Director, undertook the mission with the full knowledge and cooperation of the U.S. State Department.

In early January, 1967, Ashmore and Baggs had a long private audience with Ho Chi Minh, the last granted to Americans before his death, and transmitted to the State Department what amounted to Hanoi's general proposal for settlement of the conflict. In return, they transmitted to Hanoi, on the Department's behalf, a conciliatory letter intended to open up further exploration at the official level. A hard-line secret communication to Ho from the White House, however, effectively cancelled this informal exchange and later led to public recriminations between the Center emissaries and the State Department.

The fortunes of *Pacem in Terris II* thus were directly and inextricably entangled with the background maneuvering between Washington and Hanoi, and the great powers supporting the two sides. However, Ho Chi Minh kept open the possibility of representation at Geneva until the United States launched a new, heightened offensive against North Vietnam in April, lifting the previous ban on attacks against civilian populations. In the wake of Hanoi's withdrawal, the Soviet Union at the last minute also cancelled its participation.

Thus, in May, 1967, *Pacem in Terris II* convened in Geneva not only without the Chinese, but without representatives of the two Vietnams and the Soviet Union. This, in itself, stood as evidence of the critical increase in Cold War tensions in the wake of the stepped-up U.S. military effort in Southeast Asia. However, representatives of seventy nations, including the two Germanys and other Eastern European countries, were on hand to discuss with renewed urgency the theme, "Beyond Coexistence."

In his opening address U.S. Supreme Court Justice William O. Douglas described the Convocation as "a search for peace—not peace in terms of the absence of hostilities, but peace in the sense of the existence of a rule of law . . . . The idea of coexistence is not enough, for minds geared to it will not be sufficiently imaginative to handle the developing crises. Coexistence is the premise when a nation adopts boundaries, and annexing territory cannot be left to unilateral action or to conspiratorial groups. Tribunals must be designated to adjudicate those claims."

Robert M. Hutchins said that the object of the second Convocation was "not merely to continue the discussion but to direct attention to the immediate practical steps that must be taken if the world is to hold together and humanity is to survive. We are here as citizens of the world and friends of mankind. Peace through the medium of war is too dangerous a game to play. Peace through a common fear is not much safer: it has a transitory, insubstantial character . . . . To aim at the survival of all means to work for justice. The question is, how can it be achieved in a world in which national power is the object of all nations and in which the exercise of that power, in what is mistakenly called the national interest, may be met by a countervailing power, exercised under the influence of a similar mistake?"

The world had lost much ground since *Pacem in Terris I.* The Vietnam war had escalated; and the "Six Day War" in the Middle East coincided with the convocation. In spite of this, Hutchins expressed the hope that it would be possible, under the nongovernmental auspices of the Center, to create an atmosphere of exploration which would be difficult to achieve at an official meeting of governmental representatives.

There was at least one concrete gain in that regard. *Pacem in Terris II* marked the first public discussion between representatives of the two Germanys since the end of World War II. Their participation on a basis of full equality at the Convocation was greeted by the European press with headlines. In his presentation, Dr. Gerald Götting of the German Democratic Republic enumerated several points that would form the basis for normalizing relations between the two Germanys: the signing of a treaty to exclude violence between the two states; acknowledgement of existing frontiers; reduction of armaments by both; participation by both in an atom-free, expansible European zone; establishment of diplomatic relations not only between the two governments themselves, but among each and the other members of the international community. Dr. W.W. Schutz of the Federal Republic of Germany stressed the need for an end to East-West confrontation to be followed by East-West cooperation, and European integrations.

Also, there was a spontaneous grouping of the nations of Southeast Asia, less the two Vietnams, under the leadership of Brigadier General Said Uddin Khan of Pakistan, who had been head of the U.N. peacekeeping mission in Indonesia. There was discussion of a neutralized Southeast Asia, independent of both China and the United States, looking to development under a multilateral aid program channeled through the United Nations. Participants included leaders from Thailand, Cambodia, Laos, Malaysia, Singapore, Indonesia and the Philippines. The Center was asked to arrange a follow-up conference in Southeast Asia. General Khan later visited the countries concerned on the Center's behalf, but reported that no such conference would be practical until the fighting in Vietnam had actually terminated. Thus, five years later, the matter stands as a call for action based upon the agreement in principle summarized by Thailand's Foreign Minister Thanat Khoman: "We live in a period of transition from colonialism to a new order marked by cooperation and partnership. We do not follow Western concepts. The West cannot shape our destiny. What is required today is the cooperation of small nations. This is the true solution to peace among nations."

Pacem in Terris II concentrated on the problem of economic development. The most severe challenge to existing bilateral aid arrangements, and even the efforts of the United Nations and its specialized agencies, came from a Latin American, Dom Helder Camara, Brazilian Archbishop of Olinda and Recife. The Archbishop spoke against Latin American oligarchs and those who keep them in power: "Any economic system that assures prosperity only to a small group precludes victory over 'our internal colonialism, our national slavery.'" He added that it is not enough to "legislate beautiful laws . . . What is needed is moral pressure, democratic but strong, in order to subdue the feeble morals of the rich."

Multinational corporations and cartels also came under Dom Helder's attack: "Private initiative is becoming every day more submerged in international trusts, which are the true masters of the world." Later the Archbishop called for anti-trust legislation "on an international scale."

There was a general agreement on a number of points:

1) The colonial era must come to an end, not only politically but also economically;

2) The developing nations need aid, but this aid should be given multilaterally rather than bilaterally;

3) To this end, a new means of transfer should be set up, as suggested by the *Populorum Progressio* of Pope Paul VI, and reiterated forcefully in a special message from him to the Convocation. The U.N. Special Fund or some other agent might serve, if financed by the members of the United Nations, through a one percent tax on their GNP, as suggested on various occasions by the French, or by savings on military budgets in the wake of arms reductions, as suggested by Pope Paul.

The Convocation again brought into focus the remarkably conservative concept of international law held by the Soviet Union and its allies. This had been demonstrated at *Pacem in Terris I,* where American and European advocates of an expanding, progressive development of transnational jurisprudence as a substitute for the use of force to settle collisions of interest found themselves aligned against an adamant communist defense of the classical, restrictive concept of the inalienable sovereignty of national states, with international relations to be carried out through traditional diplomacy, treaties, and sanctions.

During the course of *Pacem in Terris II,* however, some Eastern European representatives appeared to be moving in a new direction in their view of international law. Manfred Lachs of Poland, a Judge of the World Court, emphasized, more strongly than anyone else, the obsolescence of present international law. He urged its "adaptation to the great changes wrought by the scientific and social revolutions. International law does not address itself to a timeless situation but to a grim and changing reality."

PACEM IN TERRIS III
Washington, D.C., October 8-11, 1973

Pacem in Terris I demonstrated the degree to which a new interdependence among nations had begun to reshape the world and require that the sovereign powers recognize the global character of the most urgent issues confronting them. *Pacem in Terris II* was a sobering reminder of how the old national tensions nevertheless carried over into the new age, with catastrophic results insured unless the nations found the will to pass beyond the narrow, negative limits of mere coexistence. *Pacem in Terris III*, in a departure from the multinational character of the previous convocations, considered these new global requirements in specific terms of their impact on the foreign policy of a single great power, the United States.

If history is measured by generations we are at the end of the era which takes its name from the Cold War. A quarter-century has passed since the grand alliance of the second world war split apart to leave the U.S.A. and the U.S.S.R. confronting each other along the line in Central Europe where their military forces had come together in victory.

On March 12, 1947, Harry S. Truman announced that the United States would assume responsibility for military support of Greek and Turkish régimes deemed to be threatened by covert intervention from neighboring communist countries. The President acted under a formulation of the national interest, holding that "totalitarian regimes imposed on free people, by direct or indirect aggression, undermine the foundations of international peace and hence the security of the United States." Thus emerged the Truman Doctrine, with its proclamation that the choice facing every nation lay between the democratic system exemplified by the United States, and the alternative of "terror and aggression" inherent in the world-wide communist revolution supported by the Soviet Union.

Whether the Doctrine President Truman directed against the Soviet Union was a response in kind, or served to provoke one, there can be no doubt that the interaction between the two great powers has been the dominant force in international relations since the end of World War II.

Implementation of the Truman Doctrine has determined the main directions of the United States foreign policy still in effect, although already in process of modification in the wake of President Nixon's new openings to Moscow and Peking. In February, 1970, in a message to Congress titled "A Strategy for Peace," the President set forth a new Nixon Doctrine: "We will view new commitments in the light of a careful assessment of our national interests and those of other countries, of the specific threats to those interests, and of our capacity to counter those threats at an acceptable risk and cost." Previously he had redefined the national interest in terms that considerably reduced the almost limitless reach of the Truman Doctrine, and employing the new formulation to justify withdrawing United States ground forces from South Vietnam.

The new Doctrine appears to have been accepted by both the U.S.S.R. and the People's Republic of China as a response in kind to the theory of "peaceful coexistence" as propounded, and currently practiced, by both great powers.

It is against this backdrop that a new American foreign policy must emerge if there is to be one. The minimum formulation is a new balance of power which recognizes that the bi-polarity of the Cold War is no longer applicable to the actual grouping of national interests and capabilities. The great power strategists see the new geopolitical shape of the world as pentapolar, with the vast reaches of the third world still treated in practice as hinterlands of the five metropoles of the northern hemisphere—the United States, the U.S.S.R., Western Europe, China, and Japan.

However, there are those who question whether the formulation of foreign policy in the traditional balance-of-power style may be anachronistic. Professor Stanley Hoffmann of Harvard asks: Does the complex world of the more than 130 nations engaged in a bewildering variety of interstate and transnational relations lend itself to the art of diplomacy which insured, if not peace, at least moderation and some stability before and after the French Revolution?

This is the question with which *Pacem in Terris III* began. In the agenda that followed there was no disposition to denigrate the practical necessities of traditional diplomacy. It is difficult, however, to see how any conceivable rearrangement of existing power groupings can be considered other than transient. The nation-state that survives in theory as the basic unit of power politics is undergoing profound modification in practice. As far back as 1961 Henry Kissinger wrote in *The Reporter*:

> Not even the most powerful country is capable by itself of maintaining security or of realizing the aspirations of its people. One of the paradoxes of our day is that more and more nations are coming into being at the precise moment when the nation-state is becoming incapable of dealing with many of its problems and the interdependence of states is ever more obvious.

Put another way, the political forces at work in the world appear to be dominantly nationalist and therefore separatist, but they are countered by an increasingly powerful economic-technological thrust toward supranational forms. We still live in a world fashioned by the instruments of power, but the American experience in Vietnam has raised doubts that the application of these instruments any longer achieves its stated ends. Perhaps the one thing we can be sure of is that the coming era will continue the marked erosion of the basic assumptions of foreign policy planning, forcing adjustments to meet new conditions affecting in fundamental ways the manner in which nations and peoples deal with each other. These were the matters before the house at *Pacem in Terris III*.

Convocation Committee

Chairman, Harold Willens

Vice Chairmen: Henry C. Broady, Charles H. Dyson,
Daniel E. Koshland, Mr. and Mrs. George McAlmon,
Madeleine H. Russell, Albert B. Wells

Allied Products Corporation
  Charitable Fund
Dr. and Mrs. Aerol Arnold
Elaine Attias
Mr. and Mrs. Berkley W. Bedell
Mr. and Mrs. Charles Benton
Mr. and Mrs. John Benton
Louise Benton
Mrs. William Benton
E.A. Bergman
The Bydale Foundation
Carlton E. Byrne
John B. Caron
Mr. and Mrs. John Fenlon
  Donnelly
Mr. and Mrs. Sydney J. Dunitz
Asher B. Edelman
Raymond Epstein
Mr. and Mrs. Ray Evans
C.R. Evenson Foundation
Mr. and Mrs. Milton Feinerman
The Franklin Foundation
Dr. and Mrs. Charles O. Galvin
Mr. Sheldon M. Gordon
D.S. and R.H. Gottesman
  Foundation
Ms. Beth Gould
Mr. Carl M. Gould
Mrs. Joyce Gould
Mrs. Horace Gray
Mr. and Mrs. David Grutman
Mrs. E. Snell Hall
The Hartford Element
  Company, Inc.
Mr. and Mrs. George L. Hecker
Uki and Frank Heineman
Ruth and Paul Henning
Dr. and Mrs. E. Craig Heringman

Mr. and Mrs. Harrison W. Hertzberg
Norman Hinerfeld
Mr. and Mrs. Sterling Holloway
Mr. G. Bruce Howard
Mrs. McKibben Lane
Albert A. List Foundation
Mr. and Mrs. George Lord
Mr. and Mrs. Raymond D. Nasher
Frederick M. Nicholas
Mr. and Mrs. Spencer Oettinger
Patterson-Barclay Memorial
  Foundation, Inc.
Mr. Miles Pennybacker
Fred and Gertrude Perlberg
  Foundation, Inc.
Mr. and Mrs. Gifford Phillips
Phillips-Van Heusen
  Foundation, Inc.
Mr. and Mrs. Rudolph S. Rasin
Joyce Reed Rosenberg
Sarah and Matthew Rosenhaus
  Peace Foundation, Inc.
Robert and Theodore Rosenson
Mr. and Mrs. Robert F. Rothschild
Mr. and Mrs. Miles Rubin
Mr. and Mrs. Charles Schneider
Herbert M. Singer
Hermon Dunlap Smith
Carl W. Stern
Mrs. Shelby Storck
Latane Temple
Temkin, Ziskin, Kahn and Matzner
United Brands Foundation
Philip and Emma Wain Foundation
Stephen and Claire Weiner
The Williams Foundation
Mr. and Mrs. Sam Winograd
Executive Director, Peter Tagger

161

Speakers and Participants

HARRY S. ASHMORE, President and Senior Fellow of the Center for the Study of Democratic Institutions.

ALFRED BALK, Editor, *Atlas World Press Review*.

RICHARD J. BARNET, Co-founder and Co-director, Institute for Policy Studies; former official, U.S. Arms Control & Disarmament Agency.

ELISABETH MANN BORGESE, Senior Fellow of the Center for the Study of Democratic Institutions.

GEORGE BROWN, Jr., (D., Calif.) Member, U.S. House of Representatives.

HARRISON BROWN, Professor of Geochemistry, Science and Government, California Institute of Technology.

SEYOM BROWN, Senior Fellow, The Brookings Institution; Adjunct Professor, The Johns Hopkins School of Advanced International Studies.

HERSCHELLE CHALLENOR, Professor of Political Science, Brooklyn College, City University of New York.

FRANK CHURCH, (D., Idaho) U.S. Senator.

CLARK CLIFFORD, former Secretary of Defense.

JOHN COGLEY, Senior Fellow of the Center for the Study of Democratic Institutions; editor, *The Center Magazine*.

JEROME ALAN COHEN, Director, East Asian Legal Studies, Harvard Law School; Chairman, Subcommittee on Chinese Law, American Council of Learned Societies.

RICHARD N. COOPER, Provost, Yale University; former Deputy Assistant Secretary of State for International Monetary Affairs.

THOMAS E. CRONIN, former Visiting Fellow of the Center for the Study of Democratic Institutions.

JOHN PATON DAVIES, former member, China Policy Planning Staff, Department of State.

JAMES H. DOUGLAS, former Deputy Secretary of Defense; member, Board of Directors, Center for the Study of Democratic Institutions.

CHARLES H. DYSON, Chairman, Dyson-Kissner Corporation; member, Board of Directors, Businessmen's Education Fund.

GLORIA EMERSON, Fellow, Institute of Politics, John F. Kennedy School of Government, Harvard University; foreign correspondent, *The New York Times*.

SAM J. ERVIN, Jr., (D., N.C.) U.S. Senator.

RICHARD A. FALK, Milbank Professor of International Law and Practice, Princeton University.

FRANCES FITZGERALD, author, *Fire in the Lake;* recipient, National Book Award.

WILLIAM FOSTER, former Director, U.S. Arms Control & Disarmament Agency; former Deputy Secretary of Defense.

PAULINE FREDERICK, United Nations correspondent for N.B.C. News.

J. WILLIAM FULBRIGHT, (D., Ark.) Chairman, Senate Committee on Foreign Relations.

JOHN KENNETH GALBRAITH, Paul M. Warburg Professor of Economics, Harvard University; former U.S. Ambassador to India.

RICHARD N. GARDNER, Professor of Law and International Organization, Columbia University; former Assistant Secretary of State.

LESLIE H. GELB, National Security Correspondent, Washington Bureau, *The New York Times;* former Director, Policy Planning Staff, Office of the Secretary of Defense.

NORTON GINSBURG, Dean and Senior Fellow of the Center for the Study of Democratic Institutions.

ARNOLD M. GRANT, member, Board of Directors, Center for the Study of Democratic Institutions.

JAMES P. GRANT, President, Overseas Development Council; former Deputy Assistant Secretary of State.

DAVID HALBERSTAM, former foreign correspondent, *The New York Times;* author, *The Best and The Brightest.*

MORTON H. HALPERIN, Senior Fellow, The Brookings Institution; former Deputy Assistant Secretary of Defense.

JOHN LAWRENCE HARGROVE, Director of Studies and Acting Executive Director, American Society of International Law.

THE REVEREND THEODORE M. HESBURGH, C.S.C., President, University of Notre Dame; Chairman, Overseas Development Council.

STANLEY HOFFMANN, Professor of Government, Harvard University.

RICHARD HOLBROOKE, Managing Editor, *Foreign Policy.*

DAVID HOROWITZ, Editorial writer, *Ramparts* magazine.

HUBERT H. HUMPHREY, (D., Minn.) U.S. Senator; former Vice-President of the United States.

ROBERT M. HUTCHINS, Chairman of the Center for the Study of Democratic Institutions; former President, University of Chicago.

HENRY M. JACKSON, (D., Wash.) U.S. Senator.

NEIL JACOBY, Associate of the Center for the Study of Democratic Institutions; Professor of Business Economics and Policy, Graduate School of Management, U.C.L.A.; former Economic Adviser to Presidents Eisenhower and Nixon.

PHILIP C. JESSUP, former Judge, International Court of Justice; former Professor of International Law, Columbia University.

STANLEY KARNOW, Contributing Editor, *The New Republic.*

ALEXANDER KING, Associate of the Center for the Study of Democratic Institutions; Director-General of the Organization for Economic Cooperation and Development, Paris.

HENRY A. KISSINGER, U.S. Secretary of State.

EDWARD M. KORRY, President, United Nations Association; former U.S. Ambassador to Ethiopia and Chile.

EDWARD LAMB, Chairman, Lamb Enterprises; member, Board of Directors, Center for the Study of Democratic Institutions.

GENE R. LaROCQUE, Director, Center for Defense Information; Rear Admiral (Ret.), U.S. Navy.

MORRIS L. LEVINSON, President, Associated Products; member, Board of Directors, Center for the Study of Democratic Institutions.

SOL M. LINOWITZ, Chairman, National Council of the Foreign Policy Association; former U.S. Ambassador to the Organization of American States.

PETER IRVIN LISAGOR, Chief, Washington, D.C. bureau, Chicago *Daily News.*

FRANCES McALLISTER, Member, Board of Trustees, Center for the Study of Democratic Institutions.

EUGENE J. McCARTHY, former U.S. Senator from Minnesota.

GEORGE McGOVERN, (D., S.D.) U.S. Senator; Democratic nominee for President of the United States.

HANS J. MORGENTHAU, Leonard Davis Distinguished Professor of Political Science, City University of New York.

F. BRADFORD MORSE, United Nations Under-Secretary for Political and General Assembly Affairs.

EDMUND S. MUSKIE, (D., Maine) U.S. Senator.

FRED WARNER NEAL, Associate of the Center for the Study of Democratic Institutions; Professor of International Relations and Government at the Claremont Graduate School, Claremont, California.

SENIEL OSTROW, President, Sealy Mattress Company; member, Board of Directors, Center for the Study of Democratic Institutions.

J.R. PARTEN, Vice-Chairman, Board of Directors, Center for the Study of Democratic Institutions.

PETER G. PETERSON, Vice-Chairman, Lehman Brothers; former Secretary of Commerce.

GERARD PIEL, President and publisher, *Scientific American;* recipient, UNESCO Kalinga Prize.

BERNARD RAPOPORT, President, American Income Life Insurance Company; member, Board of Directors, Center for the Study of Democratic Institutions.

GEORGE E. REEDY, Dean and Nieman Professor, College of Journalism, Marquette University; former White House Press Secretary.

EDWIN O. REISCHAUER, Professor of International Relations, Harvard University; former U.S. Ambassador to Japan.

ABRAHAM RIBICOFF, (D., Conn.) U.S. Senator.

LORD RITCHIE-CALDER, Senior Fellow of the Center for the Study of Democratic Institutions.

NELSON ROCKEFELLER, Former Governor of New York; former Assistant Secretary of State.

JONAS SALK, Director, Institute for Biological Studies; Adjunct Professor in Health Sciences, University of California at San Diego.

MARSHALL SHULMAN, Director, Russian Institute, Columbia University.

RONALD STEEL, former U.S. Foreign Service Officer; Visiting Lecturer, Yale University.

ELEANOR B. STEVENSON, member, Board of Directors, Center for the Study of Democratic Institutions.

JEREMY J. STONE, Director, Federation of American Scientists.

WALTER S. SURREY, Adjunct Professor, Fletcher School of Law and Diplomacy, Tufts University.

PAUL M. SWEEZY, former Visiting Professor of Economics, Harvard University; Editor, *Monthly Review.*

KENNETH W. THOMPSON, former Vice-President, Rockefeller Foundation.

JAMES CLAUDE THOMSON, Jr., Curator, Nieman Fellowships for Journalism.

ROBERT W. TUCKER, Professor of Political Science, The Johns Hopkins University.

REXFORD G. TUGWELL, Senior Fellow of the Center for the Study of Democratic Institutions; member of President Roosevelt's "Brains Trust"; former Governor of Puerto Rico.

STANSFIELD TURNER, Vice Admiral, U.S. Navy; President, Naval War College.

SANDER VANOCUR, Director, Communications Project, Duke University; Consultant, Center for the Study of Democratic Institutions.

PAUL C. WARNKE, Chairman, Board of Visitors, Georgetown University School of Foreign Service; former Assistant Secretary for International Security Affairs, Department of Defense.

HARVEY WHEELER, Senior Fellow of the Center for the Study of Democratic Institutions.

JOHN WILKINSON, Senior Fellow of the Center for the Study of Democratic Institutions.

GEORGE F. WILL, Chief, Washington, D.C. Bureau, *National Review*.

HAROLD WILLENS, Chairman, Factory Equipment Corporation; Chairman, Businessmen's Education Fund; member, Board of Directors, Center for the Study of Democratic Institutions.

ALBERT WOHLSTETTER, University Professor of Political Science, University of Chicago.

HERBERT YORK, Professor of Physics, University of California at San Diego; Science Adviser to Presidents Eisenhower and Kennedy.

CHARLES W. YOST, President, National Committee on U.S.-China Relations; former U.S. Ambassador to the United Nations.

About the Editors

Mary Kersey Harvey is editor of *Center Report*, a bi-monthly publication of the Center for the Study of Democratic Institutions. Previously she was an editor and writer for *The Saturday Review* and *McCall's* and director of the McCall Publishing Corporation Editorial Committee. Mrs. Harvey has lived and worked in both Mainland China and the Soviet Union, in the latter country as coordinator of several "Dartmouth" conferences of Soviet and American public figures. She has served as vice-president of a Washington, D.C. public relations firm, as consultant to the magazine division of Carl Byoir Associates, and to the nationally-televised program, "The Advocates."

Fred Warner Neal, a Center Associate and professor of International Relations and Government at the Claremont Graduate School, California, holds degrees in Economics and Political Science and was both a Nieman and Littauer Fellow at Harvard. Following war-time service, Mr. Neal became a consultant on Soviet affairs to the State Department and later chief of its division of Foreign Research on Eastern Europe. In 1950, he was a Fulbright Research Scholar at the *Institut de Sciences Politiques* in Paris and in 1961-1962 a Fulbright professor at the universities of Lyons and Strasbourg. A former correspondent for the *Wall Street Journal*, Mr. Neal has dealt extensively with the Soviet Union and Eastern Europe as a naval officer, diplomat and scholar. His most widely-known books are *Titoism in Action; U.S. Foreign Policy and the Soviet Union* (a Center publication); *Yugoslavia and the New Communism; War, Peace and Germany*, and *The Role of Small States in a Big World*. Mr. Neal has been instrumental in organizing the Center's three *Pacem in Terris* Convocations.

The Convocation in Sound

The *Pacem in Terris III* convocation, the source for these volumes, was recorded on tape from which the Center has edited a series of 28 audio programs. With the added dimension of sound, you can experience the excitement of the convocation almost as if you had been present. You will hear the interplay between speaker and audience—Senator Sam Ervin's distinctive North Carolina drawl—the demonstrators who twice interrupted the speech of Secretary of State Henry Kissinger—the incisive understatements of John Kenneth Galbraith.

The programs can be used in parallel with the printed volumes to great advantage, particularly in classrooms and discussion groups. They include off-the-cuff remarks and other departures from prepared texts that give valuable insights into the personalities and thinking of the remarkable group of men and women who spoke at *Pacem in Terris III*.

The programs in this series vary in length from 23 to 59 minutes and are available on cassettes or open reels at 3¾ ips. Prices range from $8.50 to $12.00. For a brochure describing the series in greater detail, please write to: Audio Programs, The Center, Box 4446, Santa Barbara, California 93103.

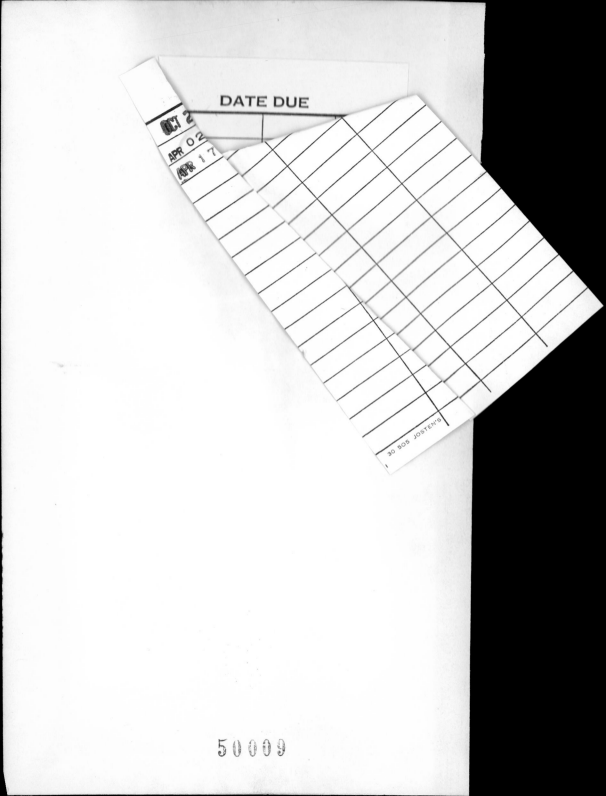

DATE DUE

OCT 2

APR 0 2

APR 1 7

30 505 JOSTEN'S

50009